2/00

with
Coping

SATANISM
RUMOR, REALITY, AND CONTROVERSY

Allen Ottens, Ph.D., and Rick Myer, Ph.D.

THE ROSEN PUBLISHING GROUP, INC./NEW YORK

Published in 1994, 1998 by The Rosen Publishing Group, Inc.
29 East 21st Street, New York, NY 10010

Revised Edition 1998

Library of Congress Cataloging-in-Publication Data
Ottens, Allen J.
    Satanism : rumor, reality, and controversy / Allen Ottens and Rick Myer.
    p. cm.
    Rev. ed. of: Coping with Satanism. 1993.
    Includes bibliographical references and index.
    Summary: Presents arguments for treating teen satanic worship as a mental health problem rather than a religious issue and provides information about rituals and symbols, signs of involvement, and the controversy surrounding this topic.
    ISBN 0-8239-2711-3
    1. Satanism—Psychology—Juvenile literature. [1. Satanism. 2. Mental health.] I. Myer, Rick. II. Ottens, Allen J. Coping with satanism. III. Title.
BF1548.0885   1998
133.4'22—dc21   98-16571
                                                              CIP
                                                              AC

Manufactured in the United States of America

About the Author

Allen J. Ottens received his doctorate in counseling psychology from the University of Illinois. He was formerly a staff psychologist in the Psychological Services Clinic of Cornell University and at the Villanova University Counseling Center. He is currently an associate professor in the Department of Educational Psychology, Counseling, and Special Education at Northern Illinois University.

Dr. Ottens is a licensed psychologist and a member of the American Psychological Association. He has published articles in the Journal of Behavior Therapy and Experimental Psychiatry and the Journal of Counseling and Development, among others.

Rick Myer is a licensed psychologist who earned his Ph.D. in counseling psychology from Memphis State University. Dr. Myer also holds a Master of Divinity degree from the Southern Baptist Theological Seminary in Louisville, Kentucky, and has worked as hospital chaplain.

Dr. Myer is an associate professor at Northern Illinois University in the Department of Educational Psychology, Counseling, and Special Education. His primary interests are crisis intervention and assessment.

Contents

Introduction:
Searching for Answers

Catherine is a sophomore living with her divorced mother and younger brother in a medium-sized city in the Midwest. She has a few good friends in high school and has just accepted a date with one of them to the annual sophomore Harvest Dance. Her grades are pretty good, and she likes most of her classes.

But like most high school students, Catherine feels a lot of pressure to fit in. She wants to be accepted, but it's hard. Sometimes she feels that she is at the center of things; at other times she feels as if she is on the outside. Sometimes she feels that she needs to be something she's not just to be accepted, instead of feeling free to be herself.

Catherine is also trying figure out what kind of person she wants to be. Does she want to be friends with the cheerleaders and the athletes, or with the drama club people, or maybe with the people who smoke behind the school? Could she be friends with all of them, she wonders.

At the beginning of the school year, Catherine's school district and another district were merged. Four of Catherine's new classmates were kids who stood out. It was rumored that they were involved in some kind of "ritual practice," perhaps Satanism. Some of

1

Catherine's friends had even heard that the new students used drugs and got the money to pay for them by stealing or dealing.

One of the new arrivals, a girl named Rikki, was assigned a locker next to Catherine's. Catherine was surprised by her appearance. Rikki's gothic wardrobe consisted of skintight leathers, chains, and drug paraphernalia-type jewelry. She wore black lipstick and nail polish and ghoulishly white foundation makeup. She had inked the design of a barbed-wire bracelet around her left wrist and was not bashful about displaying the knife and razor cuts across her legs, forearms, and midriff. Her hair had been dyed black. Her locker door sported dark, foreboding posters of some hellish-looking mythical figure in heroic poses and what Catherine thought were satanic symbols. At the same time that Catherine felt a little intimidated by Rikki's appearance, she found it fascinating. She wondered what made Rikki tick.

Catherine was also interested by Rikki's behavior. Around boys she used profane language and struck sexually suggestive poses. She seemed totally unconcerned by teachers' criticisms or comments.

That's what Catherine found most intriguing about Rikki: how little she seemed to care about "good behavior" and the opinions of others. Catherine had been taught to be polite and respectful and to take schoolwork and her elders seriously. Rikki flouted all this with obvious contempt. Catherine was conscious of the impression she made on people and cautious not to offend. Rikki's style was to invite attention and controversy.

Rikki was a frequent topic of conversation in Catherine's circle of friends, who often ridiculed Rikki behind her back. Catherine was reluctant to join in, perhaps because her feelings toward Rikki were so mixed. Despite the initial unease she had felt, Catherine also felt a tinge of jealousy. Rikki's freedom and apparent lack of inhibitions appealed to Catherine. But Catherine also felt some fear, at an unspoken level, that some of Rikki's behavior might influence Catherine herself. What if Rikki really were a Satanist?

Several of Catherine's classmates assumed that because of Rikki's clothing, behavior, and the decorations on her locker and notebooks, she was involved in Satanism. In fact, Rikki was using expressions of nonconformity to communicate something. But her message was not "I am part of a satanic cult" but "I don't accept your rules or your judgment of me." Like Rikki, some people who make use of elements associated with Satanism, such as particular symbols, are not Satanists.

Others do follow Satanism, and the ideas of Satanism shape their worldview. Some professionals believe that teenagers who experiment with Satanism are expressing normal feelings and dealing with tough developmental issues—separation from their parents, coping with low self-esteem, learning to handle rejection, and acquiring a sexual identity—but are doing so in unhealthy ways.

A Difficult Topic

Why are you reading a book about Satanism? What motivated you to pick it up? What do you hope to learn from it?

Perhaps you're curious about the topic. That's not unusual; many people are curious about unusual or fantastic topics. Perhaps, like Catherine, you know someone who seems to be connected with a satanic group. Perhaps you want more information before you decide whether to accept or reject claims about Satanism that you've heard on the news or from friends.Whatever your reason, it is useful to read the entire book in order to get a balanced perspective.

This book presents information and opinion about four areas. First, it discusses the history of Satanism, describing some satanic organizations, rituals, signs, and symbols. Second, it sheds light on the mental-health aspects of Satanism: Who is at risk of becoming involved? What motivates someone to get involved or to stay involved? Third, the book touches on some of the controversy surrounding the issues of satanic ritual abuse, recovered memory, and conspiracy networks. Finally, it discusses what you can do if you become involved in Satanism and want to break free of it.

Concerns About Satanism

In recent years, newspaper accounts and testimony by many so-called experts have often painted a shocking picture of rampant satanic activity in the United States. The reports suggest that Satanism is spreading from town to town, with satanic cult members recruiting new members and involving them in activities ranging from secret ceremonies to human sacrifice.

If we are to have a clear idea of Satanism, it is important to look at the claims and activities commonly associated with Satanism and to distinguish between those claims that are supported by evidence and those that are not.

Curiosity and Experimentation

Rikki's use of satanic symbols, gothic wardrobe, and sexually suggestive behavior had more to do with her desire to shock classmates, teachers, and parents than with a belief system involving Satanism. Many teenagers wonder about rebellious behavior and attitudes. Catherine, who has always done her best to behave well and politely, is curious to know what it would be like to act like Rikki and cause the reactions that are provoked by extreme behavior and dress.

But curiosity about rebellion can lead to confused feelings. Teenagers are trying to figure out their identities and values. Should they behave as their parents taught them to, or should they experiment with riskier identities? Some teenagers seek to expand their world by identifying with pop stars or bands. Others experiment with activities that have been forbidden by their parents, such as drug use and sex. Some teenagers intentionally date or hang out with people their parents don't approve of.

This can lead to a form of role-playing in which a person creates an identity for himself or herself that crosses behavior boundaries that have been set by adults. Using or wearing satanic symbols may be a teenager's way of remaking himself or herself to test the reactions he or she receives as a result of a new identity, according to Gary Alan Fine and Jeffrey Victor, authors of the article "Satanic Tourism: Adolescent Dabblers and Identity Work." In this way, they suggest, satanic symbolism is sometimes used by teenagers who are curious to find out what shocks and disturbs adult authorities the most.

Legend Trips

At a quarter of midnight DeAndre and Jackson met Clark, Shanda, and Lynn at the entrance to Lost Man Cave. Shanda felt scared and wanted to leave, but the others talked her into staying.

Twenty years ago a young couple had been murdered in the cave. A drifter was caught and had confessed to the crime. He told the sheriff that he had killed the teenagers to hear them scream.

Local legend had it that each night at the exact time of the murder, screams could be heard echoing inside the cave.

DeAndre lit a candle and placed it in the middle of the cave's floor. He instructed the others to turn off the flashlights and sit in a circle around the candle. The flickering light cast eerie shadows on the walls around them.

"It's almost time," Jackson told them. They held hands and stared at the candle flame. The silence in the cave was heavy as they waited to hear the screams of the doomed teenagers.

Teens sometimes participate in legend trips. A legend trip involves the testing of a local legend, such as a haunted house, cemetery, or other location linked to the supernatural or paranormal. These trips are usually not an expression of belief in such powers, but a form of entertainment.

Occasionally legend trips involve criminal activity, such as trespassing, vandalism, illegal drugs, or alcohol. Breaking rules enhances the sense of excitement and danger felt by the participants.

Legend trips are often mistaken as signs of satanic cult activity. Altars, candles, and other paraphernalia believed to be associated with satanic rituals are often found in isolated sites where legend trips are taken. Law-enforcement officials, reporters, and health-care workers are among those who have sounded the alarm about how these items are proof of the spread of satanic practices.

But even though many people believe that these remnants are evidence of satanic cult activities, the teenagers involved rarely see these trips as anything more than a pleasantly scary way to spend a Saturday night.

Music

Many parents and educators are concerned by the offensive quality of some popular music. Marilyn Manson and other performers use explicit lyrics about themes commonly related to satanic ideas: the dark side of life, despair, hopelessness, worthlessness, vampirism, suicide, homicide, evil. Parents' and educators' concerns are linked to the fact that popular music is so influential among teens.

In the United States, the constitutional right to free speech prevents the government from silencing citizens who disagree with its policies. But it also means that people can be exposed to many things that they would prefer not to hear or believe are harmful to hear. U.S. law gives listeners and readers the responsibility for choosing what they listen to and read.

Claims have been made that lyrics of some songs contain messages of hate and destruction, which brainwash listeners into becoming Satanists. A question that concerns many people is whether the music has the ability to influence listeners to engage in aggressive or self-destructive behavior.

But it would be a mistake to jump to the conclusion that someone involved in serious criminal activity is motivated by the music he or she prefers. The criminally aggressive teenager may have a preference for music that could be considered offensive to some; but most social psychologists point out that it is a preexisting tendency toward aggressive behavior that may shape the music preferences of a criminally aggressive teenager. In other words, suggests Jeffrey H. Goldstein, author of *Aggression and Crimes of Violence,* the aggressive teenager who tends to commit crime or violence may prefer music that promotes violence because it is expressive of the hostility he or she is already feeling.

Nationwide Conspiracy Theory

More alarming than claims of Satan-inspired criminal activity among teenagers and disturbing lyrics in music is the claim that a satanic cult network is operating in this country and is responsible for a wave of unspeakable crimes. What makes this claim especially remarkable is the allegation that members of this satanic network are leaders in our communities. Some Satanists, according to the claims, hold jobs in day-care centers and preschools, and others hold positions of power in government. The theory suggests that many people have been victims of these Satanists and have been used in their satanic rituals.

These claims of highly organized criminal activity among a secret society of Satanists are rarely supported by reliable evidence. Yet they are significant because they exploit the fears and anxieties of many people. According to Jeffrey Victor, author of *Satanic Panic,* misleading claims and "rumor-panics" about satanic criminal activity may be symptoms of other problems in our society.

Some experts conclude that because of the nationwide conspiracy theory, innocent people have been falsely accused of satanic ritual crimes. They also think that a number of people who believe that they are survivors of cult abuse may have had a false memory planted by a mental-health professional who is overeager or inadequately trained. The controversy over this subject continues.

Satanic Activity or Rumor-Panic?

A bunch of teenagers in western New York State were reported to have participated in satanic cult activity on Friday, May 13, 1988. This story created much commotion in the little community of Jamestown, New York. Jeffrey Victor set about investigating the alleged event. After intensive interviewing and study, Victor concluded that the story was not based on fact but was the result of a rumor-panic.

Victor found that similar rumors were circulating at the same time in various small towns over a 250-square-mile area of New York State and northwestern Pennsylvania. He also discovered that the rumors first appeared after several television talk shows had aired the topic of Satanism. Over several months, as stories of satanic activity spread, they became more and more elaborate. In time, the stories became a part of the local gossip in the small communities of the region.

What Victor discovered was a gradual process of distortion. A story from a believable source (television talk shows) became distorted through repeated retelling and became part of the local lore.

Many Jamestown residents did not believe it when the police, newspapers, and school authorities later called the story about satanic activities a hoax. These residents were convinced that the police, journalists, and educators were all in on a cover-up of the facts.

Victor's research turned up twenty-one sites in different parts of the country where rumor-panics about satanic cults had taken hold. He found that the rumors were often strikingly similar. One said that members of a satanic cult killed animals during secret ceremonies in the woods. Other rumors were variations on similar themes, such as how one or more teenagers had been selected to be sacrificed. The rumor-panics all occurred in small, rural towns in economically depressed areas. Victor believed that the people were consequently under a lot of stress and therefore more likely to be attentive to and worried about any new threats to their families.

In some of these communities, Victor noted, police departments also fell victim to the rumors and passed them along as fact. He cited a case in New Hampshire. Police claimed that they had found carcasses of "ritually slaughtered" animals in the woods. It turned out that the animals were actually road-kills that had been picked up by highway workers and dumped in the woods.

Victor's investigations suggest that the rumor-panics regarding Satanism share some similarity to "urban legends," stories repeated so often that they become local or cultural truth despite the absence of witnesses. Two examples of urban legends may be familiar to you. One is the story about how someone flushed baby alligators down a toilet and now monster alligators are living in the city's sewers. Another is the tale is of the "phantom hitchhiker" who is picked up by a motorist; moments later the hitchhiker vanishes, even though the car never stopped.

We are faced with the question of whether the claims about satanic crime are fact, rumor-panic, or something else.

Exploring the Matter

When one looks closely, the evidence suggests that much of what is alleged to be satanic cult activity is something else. Teenagers may be experimenting with rebellious or nonconformist behavior or may be entertaining themselves with legend trips or other "spooky" activities that are suggestive of Satanism; but most do so without involving themselves in the worship of Satan or any other genuinely satanic rituals. While it is true that the music we listen to can influence us, the overwhelming majority of teens can listen to music with dark content without becoming Satanists. Claims of widespread ritual cult abuse, as horrifying as they are, are not usually supported by the evidence one would expect to find.

This does not mean that Satanism and Satanists do not exist. They do, and some Satanists have been known to offer human sacrifices. It does mean, however, that much of what is commonly understood as being satanic cult activity is not. It also means that many people rumored to be Satanists, like Rikki, are not.

The next chapter concerns the question of what Satanism is.

The History of Satanism

The best way to begin our journey into understanding Satanism is to learn about its historical roots. By providing facts, this chapter seeks to dispel some of the mystery surrounding Satanism.

Satan

Satan's Names

In his book *Lucifer: The Devil in the Middle Ages,* Jeffrey Burton Russell explains that the word Satan is derived from the Hebrew word *shatan,* meaning adversary. Satan is most prominently mentioned in the Old Testament Book of Job. There Satan goes before God and challenges Job's faith. In an effort to discredit God and Job, Satan argues that Job's faithfulness is entirely dependent on his prosperity and wealth. With God's consent, Satan is allowed to play the adversarial role in bringing disaster upon Job.

In the New Testament, the Greek word *diabolos,* a translation of the Hebrew *shatan,* is used. *Diabolos* is usually translated as "devil" and bears such meanings as slanderer and tempter. Jesus' temptations in the desert following his baptism in the Jordan River are an example of the role *diabolos* was thought to play: that of tempting and persecuting humankind and causing illness, suffering, and death. As a result people began to believe that the "devil" used deceit, playing tricks to turn people away from God.

Three ancient cultures had a figure that resembled the present-day concept of Satan. In each instance, this figure was identified with a mythological underworld, the realm of the dead. Set, the Egyptian god of evil and the underworld, resembles Satan. The Greeks called their god of the underworld Hades. For both the Egyptians and Greeks, the underworld was less identified with evil than as the realm of the dead.

The most striking parallel, however, is found in Zoroastrianism, the religion of ancient Persia. This religion held that the world was divided into good and evil much as Judaism and Christianity do. But it believed in a struggle between the powers of light (good) and the powers of darkness (evil), with neither having supremacy. The powers of darkness were personified in the evil spirit Ahriman, lord of the underworld, caretaker of the wicked dead, and the great destroyer. In Zoroastrian belief, Ahriman struggles with Ahura Mazda, the power of light, for supremacy and control of the world.

The concept of the devil that developed from pre-biblical times through Jewish and Christian traditions is the devil as an obstructor of the will of God, Russell suggests in another of his books, *Satan*. Thus the devil is the personification of the principle of evil.

In Jewish and Christian traditions, the figure Satan had many names. The name Lucifer appears in the Old Testament once, and not at all in the New Testament. In Isaiah 14:12–15, Lucifer is referred to as a fallen angel because of his vanity and his desire to be God. The idea of

Lucifer as a fallen angel is referred to several times in the New Testament, but no name is mentioned. Joseph Klaits, author of *Servants of Satan,* states that Lucifer has come to be considered the emperor of infernal spirits who tempt people by appealing to their pride and selfish interests.

Beelzebub is another name for Satan found in early Jewish and Christian history. Originally a Philistine deity who was the "Lord of flies," Beelzebub became the "Lord of dung" and is called the prince of demons in the New Testament. Satan is also referred to in the New Testament as a serpent (in the Garden of Eden), and the great red dragon. Early Christians often equated worship of pagan gods with worship of the devil.

Modern-day names for Satan have also developed. "Old Scratch" has its roots in the idea that Satanism could be used to help in obtaining money and wealth. "Focalor," a lesser known name, first appeared in literature referring to Satan as a man with wings. Other names sometimes applied to Satan: the "Black Prince," "Old Horny," "Black Bogey," and "Gentleman Jack."

Satan's Appearance

Satan has been depicted in a variety of forms, most of them grotesque. Many portrayals are found in manuscripts from the Middle Ages and in cathedral sculptures and paintings. Today Satan is pictured or otherwise represented in a variety of media: album covers, books, paintings, movies, and television series such as *Millennium.*

The most popular portrayal of Satan is that of a creature that is human-like with horns, split hooves, a barbed tail,

and bat's wings. The image is probably meant to symbolize humankind's beastly lust and passions.

Other traditions hold that Satan can take any form, animal or human. Examples include black cats and black
goats. The use of black symbolizes the absence of light
and goodness. Sometimes Satan is pictured as being red or
wearing red clothing, symbolizing blood or fire. Less
often, the color green is used to portray the devil, perhaps
denoting a connection with plants and the forest. Many
portrayals include distorted and grotesque body parts to
represent Satan.

In contrast, some traditions hold that Satan is beautiful
and pleasing to the eye, the embodiment of worldly pleasures who can take the form of a handsome man or a
beautiful woman. An element of Jewish and Christian
tradition following this belief surmises that Satan uses an
attractive human form to tempt people into sin.

Tales of the Devil

Folklore and literature abound with references to Satan,
attributing various powers to him. Among notable works
of literature are Dante's *The Divine Comedy,* Vondel's
Lucifer, Milton's *Paradise Lost,* Stephen Vincent Benet's
The Devil and Daniel Webster, and C. S. Lewis's *The
Screwtape Letters.*

Many modern novels and motion pictures borrow a
centuries-old plot about a person who makes a deal with
the devil. In the original tale, Dr. Faustus, a seeker of
knowledge, used an incantation, or verbal charm, to sum-
mon Satan. Dr. Faustus traded his soul for the experience
of worldly pleasures and the possession of life's most

secret knowledge. This theme of "soul-selling" recurs throughout literature.

Some legends claim to describe how people have conjured up Satan. Some of the methods said to have been used are complex, Wade Baskin writes in *Satanism: A Guide to the Awesome Power of Satan*, but others are as simple as drawing a picture of Satan or speaking his name. In these legends, Satan is usually thought to have the ability to grant wealth, youth, beauty, or power. The price is steep: generally the person's soul after a specified time, usually seven years. To seal this deal, according to the legends, a pact is signed in blood between the devil and his victim.

In 1936 a writer of horror stories, H. P. Lovecraft, invented a black-magic spell book, *The Necronomicon*. He claimed it was written by the Mad Monk. Since then, several allegedly "authentic" versions of *The Necronomicon* have also been published.

In Europe, Satan was formerly credited with creating things that the Europeans could not explain: unique natural boulder and rock formations, and road systems, bridges, and monuments built by the Romans hundreds of years earlier. Offshoots of this folklore can be found in some American natural wonders such as the Devil's Tower in Wyoming and the Devil's Postpile in California.

Satanism

It is difficult to trace accurately the history of satanic worship before the 1800s, since prior to that time many Christians believed that *any* worship other than Christianity was satanic. We know, however, that satanic worship did occur before the nineteenth century. For instance, it is believed that the Black Mass was created in the seventh century. In addition, in the seventeenth century a fortuneteller named Catherine Deshayes held satanic worship services that involved blood sacrifices. Deshayes was burned at the stake for her activities.

Modern-day Satanism developed in the late nineteenth century in Great Britain and France, at a time when the influence of Jewish and Christian beliefs was declining. The structure of society was changing. The Industrial Revolution had begun. A new socioeconomic class, the proletariat or working class, was emerging. Its emergence threatened the old social order. Society's traditional morals were questioned. Experimentation with various beliefs was on the rise. Decadence became fashionable. All these factors played a part in the rise of occultism during this time. But it was not until the early twentieth century that the worship of Satan was publicly acknowledged.

Contemporary Satanism

Today, practices and beliefs among groups and individuals who claim to be satanic vary widely. Some groups use one scripture, some another. Many Satanists come up with their own practices, rituals, and conjurations. Some satanic groups do not take seriously other groups that call themselves satanic.

There is no single system of beliefs that all agree defines Satanism. Overall, however, one can say that Satanists tend to believe that no absolute moral code exists, that the individual and his or her personal rights should be elevated over those of the group, and that Christianity is wrong.

Satanism often appeals to a person's reason and intellect and often implicitly or explicity condemns faith as part of "weak-minded" traditional religious practice. In addition, according to some Satanists, the name "Satan" is associated with power, sexuality, individualism, and control over one's own destiny.

Following are several contemporary groups that are considered satanic. Even among Satanists, however, there is disagreement as to which groups are truly satanic.

Ordo Templi Orientis

Aleister Crowley (1875–1947) is a well-known figure in the recent history of Satanism. Some even consider him to have launched modern-day Satanism. Crowley's association with the occult began when he joined the Order of the Golden Dawn. A secret society similar to the Freemasons, the Order believed that people could learn to use cosmic forces to achieve their desires, a practice called "magick." During his association with this group, Crowley was accused of sexual acts with minors, substance abuse, and murder.

Ousted from the Order, Crowley became part of another group, the Ordo Templi Orientis, or Order of the Temple of the Orient. Originally founded in Germany, the Order had a British branch, of which Crowley became the head. The Order, which still exists, is an occultist, neopagan group violently opposed to Christianity.

Crowley came to believe himself to be the Beast named in the Book of Revelation. He also adopted a twisted version of the Golden Rule: "Do what thou wilt, shall be the whole law." He claimed to know how to make himself invisible and to possess the secret of eternal youth. Crowley died at age seventy-two. His body was cremated in Brighton, England.

The Church of Satan

Another person closely associated with Satan worship is Anton Szandor LaVey (1930–1997). Born Howard Stanton Levy, he was founder and a high priest of the Church of Satan, which he began in the 1960s.

LaVey worked for a while as a circus and carnival performer before attracting a small occult following in California. The Church of Satan encouraged free love, experimentation with drugs, and other anti-establishment views at a time when rebelliousness and hedonism were widespread among a growing segment of the population. LaVey served as a consultant to the producers of and even acted in the film *Rosemary's Baby*, a story of a woman impregnated by Satan.

LaVey wrote *The Satanic Bible*, one of the scriptures of the Church of Satan, and published it in 1969. The basic ideas of *The Satanic Bible* are expressed in the Nine Satanic Statements, all of which are antithetical to Judeo-Christian teachings. The Church redefines Christianity's seven deadly sins—greed, pride, envy, anger, gluttony, lust, and sloth—as virtues.

The Church of Satan is primarily a human potential movement, encouraging people to discover, use, and expand all their abilities and talents, without being limited by conventional ideas of decent behavior or concern for others. Members are cautioned, however, to recognize their limitations. They are also not to engage in violence

THE NINE SATANIC STATEMENTS

1. Satan represents indulgence, instead of abstinence!

2. Satan represents vital existence, instead of spiritual pipe dreams!

3. Satan represents undefiled wisdom, instead of hypocritical self-deceit!

4. Satan represents kindness to those who deserve it, instead of love wasted on ingrates!

5. Satan represents vengeance, instead of turning the other cheek!

6. Satan represents responsibility for the responsible, instead of concern for psychic vampires!

7. Satan represents man as just another animal, sometimes better, more often worse than those that walk on all fours, who because of his divine and intellectual development has become the most vicious animal of all!

8. Satan represents all of the so-called sins, as they lead to physical or mental gratification!

9. Satan has been the best friend the church has ever had, as he has kept it in business all of these years!

— From *The Satanic Bible* by Anton LaVey

or to break the law. The group practices "magic," that is, changing situations or events to match one's own will. Members are urged to study all of LaVey's writings, including, for instance, *The Satanic Witch* and *The Satanic Rituals.* Non-satanic works by Mark Twain, Niccolò Machiavelli, George Bernard Shaw, and Friedrich Nietzsche, all of whose ideas challenge conventional ideas of morality and belief, are also recommended reading. Portions of these books serve as guidelines for the sect.

The Church does not actively seek members, but waits for potential members to approach. It remains a distinct force in Satanism today, according to Larry Kahaner, author of the book *Cults That Kill.* The Central Grotto in San Francisco is its headquarters, accepting or rejecting potential members and chartering grottos around the country.

In the Church of Satan, worship is based on the belief that people need ritual, doctrine, fantasy, and enchantment. Although grottos may gather at any time, gatherings usually are held on Friday evenings. Black robes, an altar, the symbol of Baphomet (a winged, goat-like figure representing Satan), candles, bells, a chalice, wine or other pleasing drinks, a sword, a model phallus, a gong, and parchment are used to perform magic rituals. David G. Bromley and Susan G. Ainsley, authors of "Satanism and Satanic Churches: The Contemporary Incarnations," write that these rituals are of three general types: (1) sexual rituals to fulfill desire; (2) compassionate rituals to help others; and (3) destructive rituals to express anger, annoyance, and hate. Such rituals are designed to invoke Satan's name for the purpose of summoning supernatural power to effect change.

Temple of Set

This organization is a breakaway group from the Church of Satan. Michael Aquino is the best-known founder of the Temple of Set. Aquino was ordained a priest in the Church of Satan in 1971. In 1975, Aquino, who was then editor of the Church's publication, *The Cloven Hoof,* had a falling-out with LaVey. He believed the church had lost its aim. Aquino, his wife, and several other members of the Church of Satan left and founded the Temple of Set.

The Temple of Set has a number of local groups known as "pylons," over which sits the Council of Nine. In the Temple of Set, members seek to achieve self-actualization. According to Bromley and Ainsley, members believe that "the universe is a nonconscious environment possessed of mechanical consistency." Set, the Egyptian god of the night, is contrasted to the universe and sometimes violates its laws; he was formerly known by the misnomer "Satan." Members do not view Set as a god intent on evil and do not consider their theology a refutation of any major religion.

The Church of the Final Judgment

The Church of the Final Judgment, more commonly known as The Process, was founded in London in 1963 by two former members of the Church of Scientology, Robert de Grimston and Mary Anne de Grimston. It was first known as Compulsions Analysis or "The Family." The group sought to achieve unlimited personal development. Eventually, The Process believed in four gods: Christ, the male god of the waters; Jehovah, the female god of the earth; Lucifer, the male god of the air; and Satan, the female god of fire. Members believed that the world would end in about the year 2000 and that they would be saved.

Robert de Grimston was later forced out because of his apparent overemphasis on satanic themes. By 1972, the group was centered in Toronto. A year later, a portion of the members had renamed themselves the Foundation Faith of God and moved to New York. The group later moved to Arizona.

The Process is active in Los Angeles and possibly San Francisco. Police have alleged that Charles Manson and David Berkowitz, the "Son of Sam" killer, were affiliated with this organization.

Thee Satanic Orthodox Church of Nethilum Rite

Founded in 1971, Thee Satanic Orthodox Church of Nethilum Rite vehemently opposes LaVey's ideas and the Church of Satan. Members believe that God created the cosmos, including Satan, but that Satan possesses more power and knowledge than God does. Magic ritual and psychic development that allow members to access Satan's powers are part of the weekly meetings.

Kerk du Satan-Magistralis Grotto and Walpurg Abbey

According to Bromley and Ainsley, the Kerk du Satan-Magistralis Grotto and Walpurg Abbey was founded by Martin Lamers in the Netherlands in 1972. The church, located in Etersheim, received a charter from the Church of Satan in the United States. Later, Lamers moved the church and abbey to the red-light district of Amsterdam. The abbey was a bar where customers gave "religious donations" on a per-minute basis to observe "monastic sisters" dance and engage in sexual activities said to be related to religious observance. The organization ran into trouble when Dutch authorities did not accept the claim that the church and abbey could rightly be termed tax-exempt churches.

Temple of Nepthys

This organization was founded in 1975 in Novato, California. According to Bromley and Ainsley, the temple has legal status as a nonprofit church of the satanic religion. Literature prepared by the group suggests that members follow an elitist philosophy that allows them to apply "satanic principles for their own success, survival, and sexual magnetism."

Ordo Sinistra Vivendi

This group was formerly the Order of the Left Hand Path. It was founded in New Zealand by Faustus Scorpius. Its intent is to develop the full potential of each individual initiate and to bring about human self-godhood according to the group's notion of a "Faustian civilization."

The Order of Nine Angles

Based in England, its members call themselves "traditional Satanists" and claim that the group has existed for more than 100 years. They advocate a sevenfold way, encompassing seven stages of insight that can be attained by members. The purpose and teachings of the Order of Nine Angles, which is a secretive organization, are viewed by some Satanists as especially dangerous.

The Fraternity of the Jarls of Balder

Founded in 1990, this is an all-male organization that is considered by some to be satanic. It seeks to revive Western Europe's ancient heritage, including its lore, traditions, and magick. The organization has begun the European Library, a nonprofit educational source that aims to provide the modern equivalent of the Great Library of Alexandria.

Gnostics

Some Gnostics could be categorized as Satanists. Promethian Gnostics believe that Satan brought light to the world and that the creator of the world, Jehovah, is the evil deity. Dark Gnostics believe in and worship the dark force in nature.

Witches and Warlocks

A witch may be defined as a female who practices magic or sorcery; a warlock is her male counterpart. It is important to note that there are many different beliefs and ideas about Satanism and witchcraft. Not all people who claim to be witches or warlocks consider themselves Satanists. For many believers in witchcraft, there is little or no emphasis on a satanic influence. More focus is placed on the powers, both good and bad, that they believe are within each of us. Magical powers, it is believed, may take one of two forms: black magic, which is associated with evil and is used to cause harm, or white magic, which may be used to help or heal.

Other Satanic Groups

In addition to those named above, other groups that

claim to be satanic also exist. Most groups identified with Satanism are small and limited geographically. They do not give outsiders information or access to rituals. Many were inspired by the counterculture of the 1960s and the popular culture of horror found in films, music, and literature.

Information about such groups generally becomes available in one of three ways: when they become public in order to obtain tax-exempt status; when they affiliate with bookstores to sell their books and supplies; or when a member or members break the law and come to the attention of the public.

A number of former groups identified with Satanism are especially well known. Our Lady of Endor Coven of the Ophite Cultus Satanis was founded in 1948 by Herbert Sloane in Toledo, Ohio. It dissolved after Sloane's death in the 1980s. The Church of Satanic Brotherhood, a schism from the Church of Satan, was founded in March 1973 and dissolved in early 1974. The Brotherhood of the Ram was founded in Los Angeles in the early 1960s. Its members renounced other faiths and devoted themselves to Satan, considered a god of joy and pleasure. The group disbanded in the early 1970s.

The Appeal of Satanism

The modern expression of Satanism builds on humankind's historical effort to explain and justify why some things—good and bad—happen to some people and not to others. Early efforts went beyond simply trying to explain the unexplainable and to justify fate; eventually, individuals sought to exert control over the forces of fate.

Modern-day Satanists use that tradition in the attempt to control forces that will enable them to fulfill their needs and desires. The leaders are typically solitary persons, not heroic figures. They are outside the mainstream and seek to enhance their status through self-serving arcane practices.

We all have needs that we want met. The decision of how to meet those needs is up to the individual. Some may make a plan, setting goals and achieving them. Others may talk to friends or trusted adults about difficulties that they are facing. Still others turn to their religious faith for answers as to how best to cope. And others may combine all of the above. But others may turn to Satanism.

Typically, teenagers do not become involved with Satanism out of a sense of religious conviction. They usually want power to improve their status or to get something. A number of experts in the field think that these teenagers are grappling with normal feelings and difficulties but are trying to resolve them in an unhealthy manner.

For the teenager who feels he or she doesn't fit in with mainstream teen culture, Satanism may seem to offer a bond with other people who feel a similar alienation. A teenager experiencing academic failure, low self-esteem, or other personal problems may find acceptance when he or she becomes involved in a satanic cult. But if that is the reason for being attracted to Satanism, it is important to remember that there are better, healthier ways to cope with these feelings.

Satanic Symbols

Think for a moment of something that for you symbolizes an important person, place, or thing.

Did you choose your school colors? Did you think of a memento that symbolizes your love for a person?

Symbols stand for people, places, and things, especially those in which we invest loyalty, faith, pride, and devotion. We have symbols for school, country, loved ones, and religions. Because a symbol represents something that is valued, it is easy to see an attack on it as threatening, disturbing, or shocking. Imagine seeing someone scratch out the eyes of a photograph of your best friend. How would you feel? A common reaction would be rage.

When someone burns the American flag, the flag-burner is often met with contempt. Burning the American flag is not recommended. But the flag is a symbol. Fortunately, the principles on which the United States is based are stronger and more enduring than the flag chosen to symbolize them. That is why flag-burning is a constitutionally guaranteed right.

The Use of Symbols

In themselves, symbols have no power. You cannot cast a spell or conjure up the devil with them.

The symbols illustrated in this chapter, all of which are commonly associated with satanic views or Satanism, are familiar to teachers, counselors, law-enforcement officers, and mental-health professionals across the country. (Some of these symbols are used by believers of various faiths, but then they have different symbolic meaning.) When people look at them, a common reaction is disgust. Because of the symbols' associations or because of the themes that they are supposed to represent, it is easy to assume that the symbols are inherently bad.

While some use these symbols to display genuine beliefs, many people, such as Rikki, use them to communicate something other than belief in Satan.

Expressing Other Needs

You may have seen some of the symbols on heavy-metal or industrial rock albums, or as graffiti, or drawn by classmates. The symbols may be signs of satanic involvement, or they may be something else. As you look at the symbols, be aware of any feelings that rise up inside of you—disgust, curiosity, anger, amusement, fear, or embarrassment. This shows how powerful these symbols are to you.

Satanists may sport satanic symbols, but people who are not Satanists sometimes wear these symbols, too, because the symbols are in vogue. A teenager may not even be aware of any possible diabolic meaning associated with a particular symbol, but may wear it to achieve a contemporary look.

Further, Dr. Anthony Moriarty, a psychologist who has worked with teenagers involved in satanic-type activities, suggests that for many teenagers satanic symbols and

INVERTED CROSS. Since the Christian cross is considered a sign of Christian faith, an inverted cross is widely recognized as a symbol of blasphemy.

666

THE NUMBER OF THE BEAST. According to the Book of Revelation (Rev. 13:18), the "number of the beast" is six hundred threescore six and is also the "number of a man." Some believe this is a reference to the Antichrist. Thus the number 666 has become a satanic symbol.

activities do not so much represent an affiliation with Satan as they express something about the difficulties these teenagers may be experiencing. In this case, Dr. Moriarty suggests, those difficulties may cause teenagers to be drawn to Satanism—not the other way around.

In his article "Adolescent Satanic Cult Dabblers: A Differential Diagnosis," Dr. Moriarty states that the vast majority of young people who are exposed to Satanic activities or paraphernalia can be termed "dabblers." This refers to an experimental, unsophisticated, or fragmented involvement in satanic material.

Dr. Moriarty divides dabblers into three types: the *psychopathic delinquent,* the *angry misfit,* and the *pseudo-intellectual.* Dr. Moriarty has found that Satanism appeals to each of

Nema

Natas

Live

Redrum

During the Middle Ages it was believed that saying the Lord's Prayer backwards would conjure the devil. More recently, filmmakers and musicians have spelled Amen, Satan, evil, and murder backwards to suggest the invocation of dark forces.

these types for different reasons. When these dabblers use Satanic symbolism, their motives are different from what one might suspect.

The Psychopathic Delinquent

The psychopathic delinquent suffers from an extreme anti-social personality disorder. According to Dr. Moriarty, such a person is likely to be involved in drug abuse, criminal activity, and violent behavior. He or she may find that dabbling in Satanism provides an excuse for acting out hostility. The psychopathic delinquent may be attracted to Satanism as an outlet for violent, aggressive behavior, not because of any ritual or belief system attached to it. The symbols used (swastikas, skulls, etc.) are emblematic of what is really important to a psychopathic delinquent: domination of others. For such a teen, what is communicated by use of satanic symbols is the idea that abuse and domination of others is acceptable. Satanism did not cause this person's antisocial attitude; it was forming long before any involvement with satanic symbols or rituals.

Kevin

Kevin is a fifteen-year-old junior high school student. He strongly suspects (probably correctly) that as soon as he turns sixteen he will be expelled from school. To Kevin, that will not make much difference; with all his suspensions and truancies, he's rarely in school anyway.

School administrators and officials unanimously regard Kevin as a disruptive, even dangerous, influence. They are aware of his reputation for committing vandalism, theft, and other criminal acts that degrade or threaten others and of some of the cases pending against Kevin: his alleged desecration of a Jewish cemetery in which swastikas and upside-down crosses were spray-painted on headstones; his alleged theft of musical instruments from the school's band room; and his extortion of money from younger students in the restrooms and off school grounds. Kevin felt little sympathy for his victims. When questioned about the theft of the band instruments, he complained about being "harassed"

33

PENTAGRAM. This star with five points, one of which points north, is a magic symbol that represents protection and the positive elements associated with white magic. It is sometimes confused with the inverted pentagram and mistakenly used to represent black magic or Satanism.

by everyone and said that the band members "got just what they deserved" for leaving expensive instruments "lying around."

If (or when) Kevin is suspended, few students will be sorry to see him go. That's because Kevin is a loner. He doesn't trust others. If he does have a partner, it seems to be not so much for comradeship as to have someone to blame or who can provide an alibi for him.

Kevin's departure will bring a sigh of relief to many of his classmates who have been either repelled or frightened by him and his reputation. He has learned that he has an uncanny knack for disturbing and upsetting people. He thinks this is funny. Others are intimidated by him, and he likes the feeling of power over them. This power is especially enjoyable to him because he feels rejected by everyone.

INVERTED PENTAGRAM. This five-pointed star with two upright points is associated with black magic. The two upright points are thought to represent the devil's horns.

Kevin's reputed involvement in the cemetery dese-
cration and satanic activity have accentuated his aura
of unpredictability and dangerousness. It is further
underscored by the crude satanic symbols he has had
tattooed on his arm and his threatening greeting with a
"devil's horns" gesture and the words, "Hail, Natas!"
Kevin uses satanic symbolism and desecration to
assert his personal power or to mock others. He is not
inspired or motivated by Satanism. His behavior is
symptomatic of a severe conduct disorder.

In the fall of 1997, a small group of teens were charged
with the shooting deaths of students at a high school in a
Mississippi town. The teens called themselves "The Kroth."
They came together around the common desire to kill their

SWASTIKA. This ancient design signifies good fortune or luck. The arms of the swastika represent the four elements: earth, air, fire, and water. The clockwise direction of the arms suggests the spring sun and the forces of daylight. Since it became the symbol of the Nazi party, the swastika has come to signify hatred and intolerance.

enemies and practice satanic worship. Law-enforcement and judicial officials branded the group as "misfit" teenagers who viewed murder as part of a shared belief system. In the *New York Times* of October 17, 1997, a sixteen-year-old who was involved in the killings was quoted as saying, "Throughout my life I was ridiculed. Always beaten, always hated. Can you, society, truly blame me for what I do?'

The Angry Misfit
The angry misfit is a person who is boiling with rage that is directed out toward others—parents, teachers, school-mates. While this rage may be understandable, the teen has not found a healthy way to vent it and instead bottles

it up. To him or her, others are always to blame for his or her unhappiness. The angry misfit does not engage in violence, but gets in trouble because of truancy, running away, and arguing. While all teens feel left out sometimes, the misfit is often rejected by peers and feels misunderstood and lonely.

For such a teen, the attraction of satanic activity is the chance to gain acceptance from a few people who share the same angry outlook. It is not the belief system of Satanism but the camaraderie with others of a similar mindset that is appealing. When the angry misfit uses satanic symbols or body markings, he or she may be saying: "My hostility, irritability, and blaming get me rejected, except in the company of my fellow 'Satanists.' Now I belong."

Anthony and Jim

Anthony and Jim were both sick and tired of "unfair treatment" by their parents. Anthony complained of being constantly grounded and hated the rules and regulations at home. What particularly irritated him was his father's inconsistency in applying discipline. As Anthony explained it, his younger brother often "got away with murder," while Anthony was reprimanded for the slightest offense.

Jim lived with his mother and a younger sister. His mother had an alcohol problem, which left Jim with great responsibility, such as making sure groceries were purchased and getting his sister off to school. Jim was sick of having to act like "the adult" in the family; he seethed with anger at his mother's irresponsibility and incompetence.

Because of their home problems, neither Anthony nor

BAPHOMET. This half-human half-goat is an ancient symbol whose origins are lost. In the Middle Ages his horns and wicked deeds linked him to Satan. Today Baphomet is not worshiped but is utilized in occult art as a symbol of Satan. In 1966, the Church of Satan adopted as its symbol "The Baphomet": a goat's head inside an inverted pentagram outlined by a double circle.

Jim was involved in school extracurricular activities. Neither made any close friends. Teachers generally regarded them as sullen and unmotivated.

Anthony and Jim seemed to gravitate toward each

other. They recognized the bond of anger and unhappiness that they shared. They understood each other. They began to hang around together both at school and at each other's homes. As their closeness grew, they took steps to cement their friendship and make their relationship even more special. They ritually punctured each other's skin and made a blood-brothers' pact. They smoked cigarettes and drank whiskey that Jim stole from his mother's supply.

As their friendship grew, Anthony and Jim seemed to arrive almost simultaneously at a new idea to bond them together. They had watched a television program about Satanism and had glanced at some library books about it. Together they bought some black candles and incense and set up a makeshift altar in a shed at the back of Jim's yard. Here, in candlelight, they invoked Satan's name against a number of their "enemies" in school and at home. This gave them a way of getting even, of expressing their anger, and of feeling closer to a friend who felt similarly depressed and helpless. They began to put satanic symbols on their books and their lockers. Some other students began to notice their apparent involvement in Satanism.

Anthony and Jim's friendship peaked during a three-day expedition on the road as runaways. Feeling pushed to the limit, depressed, and bitter, they skipped school one day, hitchhiked, and wound up 400 miles from home before being identified by a state patrolman.

Rumors at school suggested that they ran away because of Satanism. Closer study suggests that other factors were behind it. By teaming up, Anthony and Jim could commiserate. They could rail against the unfairness of the world and join in acting-out behavior.

The Pseudointellectual

The pseudointellectual may be a bright student who is not inclined toward violence or hostility. The pseudointellectual likes to get the best of others through superior knowledge or intellect. Such a person may read many books on Satanism, acquire an impressive array of facts and vocabulary, and flaunt this knowledge to teachers or schoolmates. He or she may have a few friends who share this interest.

On the surface, this person may seem to be deeply into Satanism as a belief system, persuasively arguing the merits of satanic ritual or philosophy. What the pseudointellectual is really doing, however, is enjoying knowing more than others and feeling superior. Satanic symbolism on his or her body or clothing may be communicating: "I know something you don't know."

Liz

A few topics really interest Liz. She consumes science fiction and books about hypnotism, witchcraft, parapsychology, and the Middle Ages. Dungeons and Dragons and other fantasy games are another interest. Her parents have given up on trying to expand her interests and help her become more "well rounded." Most of her high school classmates are tired of hearing about Dungeons and Dragons and obscure facts and myths.

TALISMAN OF NECROMANCY. Necromancy is the ancient art of raising the dead for the purpose of foretelling the future. This talisman is often used in the rituals of necromancy.

For art class, Liz does pencil sketches and watercolors of exorcisms, satanic angels, and her Dungeons and Dragons fantasy character, Sir Galwynne. The same artwork fills the margins of page after page in Liz's course notebooks.

One might mistakenly conclude that Liz is being influenced by Satanism. But in psychological terms she is obsessed with fantasy. She devotes so much mental energy to her fantasies that her involvement in other activities and social relationships is impaired.

It seems that no matter what the topic of the conversation is, Liz almost always brings it back to a discussion of her obsession. Her constant references to obscure knowledge are symbolic of how she attempts to assert herself. In her personal view, by being "better" than most other teenagers, she assumes a role of importance or power.

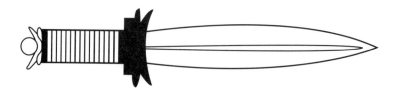

ATHAME. Knife or sword used in occult rituals, representing a person's life force and mind. The athame traditionally has a black handle and a steel blade from 4" to 8" long. Magic symbols are often painted on an athame.

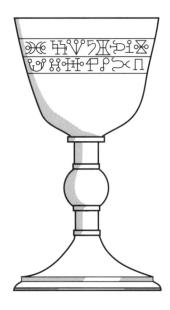

CHALICE. In magic rites, the chalice or cup represents the element of water. It is believed that a person's soul is contained in the cup. The chalice is sometimes used like a crystal ball to foretell the future.

Dungeons and Dragons

It has been alleged that fantasy role-playing games have led some teenagers into the occult, and later into full belief and membership in satanic cults. However, most experts agree that there appears to be no basis for these claims.

Critics of fantasy role-playing games allege that the games have a corrupting influence and are dangerous occult activities. They claim that the imaginary mystical characters—witches, sorcerers, denizens of the under-world—concocted during play represent unwholesome-ness. Further, say the critics, becoming engrossed in these games could cause a player to relax defenses against evil and thus could provide Satan a window of opportunity to gain control of the player's personality. Critics also claim that players who take the fantasy too seriously may give their imagination so much free rein that they lose their grip on reality and act out the violence that may be part of a particularly rousing game in real life.

Two sociologists, Daniel Martin and Gary Alan Fine, present a different perspective on fantasy games. In their article "Satanic Cults, Satanic Play: Is 'Dungeons and Dragons' a Breeding Ground for the Devil?," they assess much of the research on the topic. They conclude that fantasy role-playing games do not foster destructive behavior. To the contrary, they speculate that fantasy games may actually prevent self-destructive behavior, since teenagers may find an accepting niche in the community of their game-playing peers. Second, Martin and Fine cite studies indicating that children who engage in fantasy or imaginative activities show better social and

WAND. In satanic or magic rituals, the wand represents the element of fire and is a symbol of will, power, and strength. Magicians often make their own wands by cutting willow branches and attaching crystals or other ornaments to them.

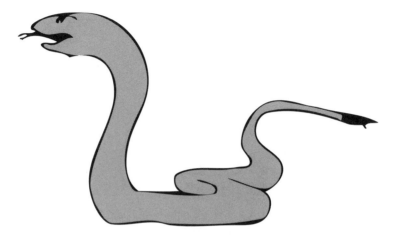

SERPENT. In Genesis 3:1–6, Eve is tempted by a serpent to eat the forbidden fruit in the Garden of Eden. The serpent represents Satan and the forces of evil.

mental development. Finally, they question whether Dungeons and Dragons truly represents a "breeding ground" for the devil, or whether the game should be viewed as a "controversial" leisure activity such as numerous other pursuits (e.g., billiards, dancing, pinball) that have been targets of disapproval.

Sending a Message

A teenager who uses or displays satanic symbolism may in fact be expressing a connection to a satanic group or an attachment to a set of satanic beliefs. More likely, however, his or her use of these symbols reveals how a teen is feeling. Teens who display such symbols may be communicating something about their hostility, their need to dominate others, or their difficulty in socializing. For that reason, it is best to avoid jumping to a conclusion about a person who displays satanic symbols, as such a conclusion will probably be mistaken.

Rituals and Ceremonies

Jerry entered an old house and walked into the "sacristy," a room that had been converted for the worship of Satan. The walls were black except for a brightly painted representation of Satan. On the floor, a star had been painted, and on each point a black candle burned. Jerry took his place at the head of the circle, making the number in the group thirteen. All members were dressed in black robes except Mary, who was wearing white. Mary moved to the center of the circle, and the initiation ceremony began. Jerry intoned a conjuration.

As Jerry spoke, five members of the circle approached Mary and removed her white robe. A long black robe was then placed on her by the remaining members. Mary was now considered a member of the family of Satan.

Satanic initiation ceremonies vary from group to group. Some groups devote much time and energy in experimentation to find the best possible combination of chants, incantations, sacrifices, and ceremonies. As a result, although rituals have similarities, unique variations are devised to meet the needs of particular groups.

This chapter covers both rituals and ceremonies. Keep in mind that these are general descriptions. Rituals and ceremonies are often altered because a group thinks it has devised something more powerful, or because it does not know—or, possibly, understand—the traditional form. Some satanic groups invent their own rituals and ceremonies.

What follows is not intended as a "how to" but as information to help you understand the mindset and goals of those who engage in satanic practices.

Rituals

In her book *Drawing Down the Moon,* Margot Adler notes that ritual appears to have a twofold purpose: first, to alter the way a person thinks by activating usually dormant parts of the mind; and second, to invoke some type of power, such as power over another person, and to give thanks. Invoking power often involves requesting something from Satan; for example, success in business, power over another person, or power to heal.

Rituals take many forms, some complex, some simple. Chants or spells may be used, as well as physical movement or offerings such as sacrifices.

Conjurations

Conjurations, or conjures, are used to call forth Satan or other demons. Incantations vary in form depending on the time of day and year. Generally they are spoken, but they may be accompanied by dancing, specific motions, or ritualistic objects believed to augment the power of the ritual.

The Great Key of Solomon is the most famous manual of magic. It contains many incantations for summoning evil spirits. Legend has it that it was written either by Solomon or by devils who hid it under Solomon's throne.

Tradition maintains that specific rules must be followed to conjure Satan and other demons. For example, some believe that Lucifer may be invoked only at dawn on Monday and provided that the conjurer wears a new stole and loose-fitting white gown and offers a live mouse as a pledge. Other demons can be summoned only at certain hours on certain days of the week.

Sacrifices

While some satanic groups consider it wrong to harm any life force, others use blood sacrifices in worship. Sacrifice of an animal, a human, or other object has been a common religious practice since ancient times. Sacrifices in Satanism often entail the use of blood, which is considered the life force and therefore very powerful. This belief is similar to Jewish and Christian traditions in which blood was also considered the power that gives life. The Bible is full of examples of the sacrificial spilling of blood as worship or symbolizing forgiveness of sin. In Satanism, sacrifices are used to demonstrate loyalty and to draw Satan near.

Several methods are used to obtain the blood needed for satanic ritual. Most often, animals such as chickens, goats, cows, roosters, white rats, cats, and dogs are used. The animals are either killed and bled or cut and the blood collected. Sometimes specific organs are used, including head, heart, liver, and sex organs of both male and female animals. Satanists believe that each organ has a particular power. The heart is considered the embodiment of the soul;

the head, the site of the spirit. The sex organs are believed to confer the power of the animal. Author Larry Kahaner observes that police reports abound of animal mutilations that are believed to be ritual sacrifices.

Although historically human sacrifice is rare, some suggest that present-day Satanists have made it a common phenomenon. A group of police officers, nicknamed the "cult cops," assert that one in ten homicides is related to Satanism, according to Kahaner. People who believe the cult is a threat to society state that more than 50,000 human sacrifices occur yearly. Other groups estimate that between 50,000 and 60,000 children are sacrificed yearly for satanic purposes. Such statistics, however, are based on belief, not fact. The FBI Uniform Crime Reporting system has no category for cult crimes. James T. Richardson, Joel Best, and David G. Bromley, authors of *The Satanism Scare,* note that sociologists attribute the estimates to the current public hysteria about Satanism.

In *Cults That Kill,* Kahaner discusses satanic beliefs followed by some. These Satanists believe that just before death a person emits a life force that can be captured and used to do the will of another person. Babies are considered to have the greatest life force because they are pure and uncorrupted. A prize possession of a Satanist is a candle made from the fat of an unbaptized baby. Fingers from the left hand are also considered very powerful and are used in rituals. The symbolism behind this belief concerns the right path of goodness and left path of evil.

The blood of sacrificial victims is allegedly used to make drinks that give power. This practice is probably a carryover from the Christian sacrament of the Eucharist, in which wine sacramentally becomes the blood of Jesus Christ. Sometimes during the ritual, blood from the sacrificed creature is smeared on Satan worshipers.

It is not known how many Satanic groups use blood sacrifices in worship. However, the Church of Satan expressly forbids violence and the breaking of state or federal law.

Sexual Magic

Satanic groups that practice sexual magic believe that the energy released during orgasm can be captured and harnessed. Aleister Crowley helped to standardize the practice of "sexual magic." He placed ads in newspapers to solicit deformed people with whom to have sex. He believed that the greater the deformity, the more powerful the sexual magic that was released.

Witches' Sabbats or midnight meetings are historically associated with sexual magic, according to author Wade Baskin. Existing accounts report that at the end of the Sabbat the people attending would remove their clothes and engage in sexual activities. Satan was said to participate by having sex with every man, woman, and child in attendance.

One myth declares that sexual magic can be used to initiate women into the service of Satan. A male member of the cult must have intercourse with a woman initiate three nights in succession, at midnight at the family burial ground.

Sexual magic has also been associated with ritual sexual abuse of children. Police throughout the country have reported such cases, often involving young children and incest victims. The accuracy of these accounts varies; in many instances the allegations have been proved false. This is discussed further in chapter 6.

Ceremonies

Ceremonies are used to give order to the many rituals used in Satanism. Information about the ceremonies is sketchy; it is believed that the ceremonies lose their power if known by outsiders.

Sabbats
Sabbats are periodic gatherings of witches, warlocks, and necromancers. Witches and warlocks do not always, however, claim to be Satanists.

Typically, Sabbats take place in secluded areas such as forests, abandoned ruins, and caves. Many colorful descriptions have survived from the Middle Ages: wild orgies, Satan and other demons flying on broomsticks, obscene sacrifices, humans changing into animal shapes, and other fantastic occurrences. Historians agree that such reports were a product of the religious controversies of the time and were sometimes used by the Church to persecute non-Christians.

Today Sabbats are generally more moderate. Those who attend say that Sabbats are used as times for performing various forms of magic and getting in touch with the meaning of life. Instead of sexual magic, sexual symbolism and poetry are used. Readings, dancing, and music are employed. Participants express deepened spiritual awareness and sensitivity to the forces of life.

Black Mass

In his book *Lucifer: The Devil in the Middle Ages,* Jeffrey Burton Russell notes that the Black Mass is an inversion of the Christian Mass. Surprisingly, it was not originally considered satanic. It is generally believed that rebellious priests initiated the Black Mass as a form of hostility toward the Church. As the Black Mass evolved over time and the rituals became more corrupt, it became the primary form of satanic worship. Since the power of God is invoked in the Mass, it was considered logical that the Black Mass would call forth the evil powers of Satan. The Black Mass arose sometime in the seventh century. In the eighth century, it became more widespread.

As the Black Mass evolved through the Middle Ages, it became more a mockery of the Christian Mass, and Satan became the object of worship. Celebration was by a defrocked priest. Participants wore long black robes embellished with satanic symbols. The altar was dominated by an obscene figure of Christ or an infernal goat. Black candles were used, along with a chalice filled with blood or human fat. A woman was sometimes used as the altar, the ceremony celebrated on her buttocks or stomach.

In the seventeenth century Catherine Deshayes, a fortuneteller also known as Madame Monvoison, was involved in a sensational criminal case in Paris. She held Black Masses for clients to cast spells for various purposes, especially to win back lovers. She also supplied clients with drugs and poisons. Ordained priests led the Masses, often reciting the liturgy backward. The blood of sacrificed or aborted babies was used instead of wine. A public executioner called LaVoisin furnished Deshayes with human fat, which was used to make black candles. Other portions of the Mass were also corrupted. The crucifix was turned upside down. Deshayes was burned at the stake in 1680 for her satanic activities.

Records of the Black Mass do not appear again until the nineteenth century, when it was revived by cults in France. From then to the present day, it has come and gone in occult tradition. The present-day celebration of the Black Mass largely follows its historical form. If a sacrifice is made, the priest offers an invocation, asking demons to accept the participants' sacrifice and give them the things they request.

At the height of the celebration a sexual orgy may take place or the officiating priest may have sexual intercourse with one or several women participants.

Satanism's rituals and ceremonies are still shrouded in mystery, and mystery often makes things more appealing. Needless to say, they should not be entered into lightly.

Holidays

Satanists observe many holidays. Not all are observed by all Satanic groups, and some groups develop their own holidays to meet their needs. One of the most important holidays of all is a Satanist's birthday.

Summary

Some people genuinely follow Satanism. They may use satanic rituals, ceremonies, and beliefs as a way to help them understand the meaning of life. However, some people take part in Satanism because they lack self-confidence and self-esteem. They use satanic worship to hide this lack of confidence or to find acceptance. Teens are most often in this category. Their reasons for joining combine the needs to camouflage feelings of insecurity and to gain recognition.

Some people use satanic rituals and ceremonies as scare tactics. Criminals and drug traffickers have used superstition and fear to pressure others to break the law. They employ satanic symbolism not to worship Satan but to send threatening messages to prospective customers. They prey on people's needs and low self-esteem for the sake of profit.

Others join satanic groups because they see Satanism as a way to avoid being responsible for their own choices. For example, someone may give up her power and responsibility to make a career choice on her own. She may sacrifice animals and have incantations made so that someone else will make the decision for her.

It is helpful and wise to seek guidance for major decisions such choosing a career, a college, or an academic major. But your adviser should be someone who will empower you to make your own decision rather than usurp your control by making the decision for you.

Two Views of
Satanic Crime

There are those who are certain that Satan exists on earth, preys upon vulnerable persons to do his bidding, and is the force behind rampant crime that is satanic in nature. There are skeptics who question the occurrence of Satan-inspired crime, question the reliability and lack of evidence of satanic crime reports, and therefore look for alternative explanations. Somewhere in between are many people who are alarmed, curious, and uncertain about conflicting claims concerning satanic crime.

The Police Model

Robert D. Hicks, a Virginia law-enforcement consultant, has assessed police activity in relation to alleged satanic crime. In his article "Police Pursuit of Satanic Crime," Hicks proposes a "police model," a model based on his findings of how police view Satanism. He does not believe that the police model is a correct view of Satanism; he cautions that it may be more a matter of speculation than fact. But the police model is important because it is the basis for much law-enforcement policy concerning suspected satanic crime. The police model suggests that there are four levels of involvement in Satanism.

First Level

The first and highest level of Satanism is said to be practiced in a supersecret fashion. One group of First Level practitioners may consist of generations of Satan worshipers from the same family. People involved to this degree come from all walks of life. They are sometimes referred to as "traditional Satanists."

These people are the "violent crime" cultists: kidnappers, murderers, and sexual offenders. Some people claim that these Satanists have formed international conspiracies dedicated to crime. The alleged victims of their crimes are children. The children may be kidnapped or forced into participating in cult practices, then sacrificed or tortured during satanic ceremonies.

The number of First Level Satanists and their victims is estimated at well into the thousands. But secrecy around this level of involvement is tight. Furthermore, no participant at this level would dare go public for fear of severe punishment or even death at the hands of the conspiracy.

A Satanic Conspiracy Network?

It is claimed that favorite targets of First Level Satanists are day-care centers and preschools. This belief seems to have arisen in the late 1970s. At that time two unrelated groups of stories were receiving a great amount of attention in the media. The first group of rumors involved the pervasiveness of child pornography in the United States.

Paralleling the child victimization allegations were reports by women who claimed to have escaped from satanic cults after having been ritually abused, most as children. Although no credible evidence was ever adduced to substantiate the reports of a conspiracy network, many people, including child protection workers, believed them. Some people began to fear that a conspiracy had existed for years and continued to threaten the welfare of children.

In the 1980s the hysteria resulting from these claims grew. Reports began surfacing in the media about astonishing types of abuse of children by their parents, day-care workers, and other adults in charge of children in various settings. A California girl accused her stepfather of forcing her to kill an infant, eat feces, and engage in ritualistic sex. In reports from Arizona and Nebraska, children claimed to have been drugged, abused, and tortured during satanic rituals. Children in other states alleged that day-care teachers performed bizarre rituals and abuses on them.

Investigation of these cases, however, has often disproved the allegations. Mental-health experts and police concluded that many of these claims were based in fantasy or on stories the children had seen or heard in the media. In the article "Problems in Multiple Victim Cases" by R. Cage, one telling case was cited. A three-year-old boy reported that a midget doctor named David had bruised his buttocks. The boy's parents suspected ritualistic abuse and notified authorities. Other children were interviewed, and as a result of leading questioning and cross-germination the reports of abuse became widespread. After careful investigation and several interviews with the boy, however, the authorities discovered that the "midget doctor" was actually a four-year-old playmate in day care.

The typical result in these day-care and school cases is that charges are dropped. In the few cases that have come to trial, the accused usually have had a history of child molestation, were themselves molested as children, or are mentally ill. The cases did not support the theory of a satanic conspiracy network.

Still, a growing number of adults reported having been victims of childhood ritual abuse twenty or thirty years earlier. Reports of recovered memory and First Level Satanic abuse are discussed in the next chapter.

Second Level

Practitioners in the Second Level are "organized Satanists" or "religious Satanists," according to the police model. These are public groups that have appeared on the scene within the past few decades. The best-known example is the Church of Satan. Significantly, Second Level practitioners view satanism as a religion that can be practiced openly rather than in a secretive fashion. In addition, although members of the groups follow Satan, the groups denounce violence and reject any connection with criminal activity.

These groups tend to believe in practices that are the opposite of traditional Judeo-Christian religious teachings. For example, the Satanist would practice indulgence (seeking pleasure) rather than abstinence (doing without) and would take revenge rather than turn the other cheek. One of their teachings exalts the potential of human beings over that of God. Police characterize Second Level practitioners generally as being unpredictable, intelligent, and curious. Because of the pleasure-seeking nature of the groups' activities, however, criminal types may be attracted.

Third Level

"Self-styled Satanists" make up the Third Level of

involvement. They may display satanic symbols or embrace a satanic ideology or philosophy, but they are people on the outermost fringes of society. Persons in this category include sensational criminals such as Charles Manson or Richard Ramirez, the serial murderer called the "Night Stalker." Ramirez achieved some publicity when at a court appearance he showed reporters a pentagram carved into his left hand. He left the courtroom that day shouting, "Hail, Satan!"

Third Level Satanists seem to use Satanism more as an excuse for criminal activity than as religious expression. They are most likely to have long-standing personality problems and to function far outside society's standards.

Fourth Level

"Ritual dabblers" or "dabblers" is a term applied to those at the Fourth Level of involvement in the police model. They usually range in age from preteens to mid-twenties. Dabblers are people who try something out without serious intent. They may not fully understand or appreciate the implications of their behavior. The overwhelming majority of teenagers who are fascinated by or involved in satanic ritual fall into this group. They are not likely to be deeply dedicated to the worship of Satan.

An Assessment of the Police Model

In recent years, law-enforcement professionals have put together presentations to alert police departments and community agencies to the threat of Satanism. The main purpose of these seminars is to heighten participants' awareness of a connection between satanic practices and criminal activity. Such presentations frequently follow the police model.

Typical of such presentations is one that was held in Des Plaines, Illinois, a Chicago suburb. Chicago Police Detective Robert J. Simandl led this six-hour seminar that included audiotapes, a lecture, and television clips. Simandl said that the seminar was targeted toward those puzzled by a rash of activity including grave robberies and cemetery desecrations, peculiar teenage suicides, ritual child molestations, mutilations, and devil-worshipers sacrificing pets and even humans while dressed in black robes. Simandl went on to say that although there are no accurate statistics regarding a connection between crime and satanic practices, the police found the Satanism theory useful in explaining baffling thefts, murders, and suicides.

Hicks, who described the police model, disagrees with Simandl and others who make such presentations. He argues that the typical law-enforcement presentation about links between satanic activity and crime is based on questionable assumptions and information. He cautions against drawing the wrong conclusions for the following reasons:

1. Hicks argues that the satanic crime seminars present the issue in a "huckster fashion," using props such as altars, skulls, occult symbols, and so forth. This theatricality exerts a powerful influence on an audience; it fosters a sense of mystery and strongly suggests that such objects are unquestionably connected with crime.

Frequently, the audience accepts the connection unquestioningly; it seems natural to associate these macabre props with unnatural or criminal behavior.

2. Hicks calls the police model of satanic crime erroneous. According to the model, it is assumed that individuals tend to progress through an increasingly involved course of satanic crime. Essentially, one starts as a Fourth Level dabbler and proceeds to First Level, engaging in supersecret satanic crime such as kidnapping, murder, and abuse, as discussed in "Dabbling Their Way to Ritual Crime" by Simandl and B. Maysmith. Hicks maintains that such a progression is unlikely, given the radical personality change required. One would have to go from enthusiasm for heavy-metal music to a capability for murder, kidnapping, and child abuse.

3. Hicks holds that there is little evidence that First Level involvement exists. At this level, activity is allegedly so supersecret that all crimes are covered up and no evidence leaks out. Crimes are said to include child abuse and human and animal sacrifices carried out by a criminal network of Satanists who are public figures such as judges, politicians, and lawyers. Hicks urges skepticism of such unseen conspiracies, since no evidence of their existence has been found. Moreover, he says it is unrealistic to believe that they could be kept secret for so many years.

Cult seminar presenters often point to two sources of evidence to prove that First Level involvement does occur: the remains of animal sacrifices, and reports of persons who claim to have undergone satanic ritual abuse. However, Hicks cites a study carried out by a former FBI agent, Kenneth Lanning, who concluded that "virtually all" reported livestock mutilations are the result of natural scavengers and predators. Reports of ritual abuse survivors are discussed in the next chapter.

4. Law-enforcement seminar presenters often quote newspaper stories to support their claims. Hicks makes the case that some of these accounts may contain unreliable reporting. For example, many newspapers ran the tragic story of a New Jersey boy who killed his mother before taking his own life. Police investigators found books on the occult and Satan worship in his room, and the press left their readers with the clear implication that the crime was inspired by the boy's Satanic involvement. Hicks argues that there are other possible explanations that the reporters never considered. He cautions that we cannot automatically connect the presence of satanic books with the criminal acts.

5. Hicks raises a question about the bias, or preconceived opinion, of the seminar presenters. He notes that a number of such police officials hold conservative Christian viewpoints. In their seminars, they sometimes borrow material from conservative Christian literature to substantiate their claims.

One such claim is the controversial notion that satanic messages are secretly dubbed into some heavy metal and industrial rock music recordings. Hicks argues that seminar presenters who hold fundamentalist religious views are likely to be biased toward those who hold different religious views. Also, Hicks is concerned that fundamentalist seminar presenters can shift the blame for criminal activity away from people and onto evil spiritual or unseen forces.

Conflicting views exist concerning the reliability of the police model and related law-enforcment views of the link between Satanism and crime. The debate on this matter continues.

The Controversy over Satanic Ritual Abuse

One of the most controversial topics surrounding Satanism is that of satanic ritual abuse, allegedly carried out by First Level Satanists. Beginning in the late 1970s, a number of women claimed to recall having been victims of such abuse, usually suffered in childhood. Most remembered the abuse when they were in their thirties or forties. This is known as recovered memory.

Sexual and physical abuse of children is a genuine societal problem. When reports of recovered memory of satanic ritual abuse began to spread, controversy developed over how much child abuse, if any, was carried out by conspiracy networks of Satanists.

Media investigation of the phenomenon led to the development of a profile of the alleged victims, according to P. Jenkins and D. Maier-Katkin, authors of the article "Occult Survivors: The Making of a Myth." Typically the person is a thirty- to forty-year-old woman who has become aware of her alleged abuse either during intensive psychotherapy or after a "born-again" religious conversion. Her memories and recollections may be recent or may go back to early childhood.

Even though victims are from widely scattered communities and the alleged abuse occurred in various regions of the country, these adults report events that are remarkably similar in detail, even down to the styles of ceremonial robes and paraphernalia used. The reports include ritual sexual acts, blood drinking, ritual murder, and cannibalism. How is such similarity possible if a satanic conspiracy network does not exist? Dr. Frank W. Putnam, on staff at the National Institute of Mental Health and author of the article "The Satanic Ritual Abuse Controversy," offers an explanation:

"Studies . . . have demonstrated that rumors, urban legends, and other folk tales can be rapidly disseminated throughout our society and are shared in common by large numbers of people who have never directly met each other. The child-abuse community is particularly susceptible to such a rumor process as there are multiple, interconnected communication/education networks shared by psychotherapists and patients alike. In addition, there is massive media dissemination of material on the satanic, through dramatic autobiographical accounts, sensational talk-shows, and news reports of alleged cases, not to mention the numerous movies and television programs that feature occult and demonic themes."

Some people have unwavering faith that a conspiracy exists. Others, however, have begun to question that idea.

Views in Support of the Idea of a Conspiracy

Following are three reports representing the satanic-conspiracy side of the controversy.

The first report is by Lynn C. Elliott, author of the article "Satanic Ritual Abuse and Multiple Personality Disorder." Elliott is a professional counselor. She notes:

"As more and more survivors begin to remember and talk, we are learning about satanic practices and victimization. In these cults, infants and children are used by cult members to align themselves with Satan and gain power. These children may actually be killed and sacrificed, systematically and ritually tortured, or sexually and physically abused for years. Children are often forced to torture or kill other children, as well as animals such as cats, chickens, and goats.

"Hypnotic techniques, drugs, trickery and illusion ('magic'), terror tactics, sleep deprivation, starvation and innumerable other abuses are used to brainwash victims and insure their compliance. Victims are also threatened that if they ever talk or try to leave the cult, they and/or others will be killed. In certain rituals, children are told they are now 'Satan's child' or that Satan is now inside them. Somewhat older children and adults may become 'Satan's bride' or may be used as 'breeders,' wherein they are repeatedly impregnated and their babies sacrificed.

"These rituals are performed and practiced according to the satanic calendar. Victims are taught that they must practice rituals involving blood and fire (often including self-mutilation), satanic symbols and objects, or magic and that they must attend cult meetings on certain dates."

The second is a report out of Canada. In an article in the Toronto *Globe and Mail* entitled "Satanic Child Abuse Cited by Aid Group," journalist K. Makin noted: "Ontario child-welfare workers have found twelve to fourteen cases of violence against children in the past three years that are related to Satanism, but politicians still refuse to look into the issue, says the director of the Ontario Association of Children's Aid Societies. George Caldwell said that although only a couple of instances have become known to the public, all of the activities and ritual sacrifices seem too authentic to be faked. 'It is so bizarre as to make you wonder whether you are going out of your mind,' he said."

The third report, written by mental-health professionals W. C. Young, R. G. Sachs, B. G. Braun, and R. T. Watkins, appeared in the journal *Child Abuse and Neglect.* The report is based on interviews with thirty-seven adults suffering from mental illnesses known as "dissociative disorders." Such disorders are characterized by disturbances in one's sense of identity. For example, a victim of a traumatic event is sometimes unable to integrate fully the traumatic experiences into his or her personality. The authors of the report write:

"All patients reported abusive rituals during Satanic worship, but reported some differences such as the color of robes worn by cult members, types of cult-related symbols and instruments, or details of rituals. The ritual abuses most frequently reported included forced drug usage, sexual abuse, witnessing and receiving physical abuse/torture, witnessing animal mutilation and killings, being buried alive in coffins or graves, death threats, witnessing and forced participation in infant 'sacrifice' and adult murder, 'marriage' to Satan, forced impregnation and sacrifice of own child, and forced cannibalism."

The following claims are typical of satanic-conspiracy reports:

↝ They refer to the victims as being subjected to bizarre crimes and abuses.

↝ They say that victims have been brainwashed, or

progammed to obey commands of cult members in robotlike fashion.

↪ They postulate elaborate ritual (and criminal) activity in which a number of people participate.

↪ They say that instances bear striking similarity to each other. Because people from different parts of the country (and therefore unknown to each other) describe similar types of abuse and ritual activities, it is asserted that the reports must be authentic.

These reports, all from apparently reputable sources, raise many questions.

Are the stories of the children to be believed? Could children lie about things so horrible? Are their reports the result of overactive imaginations? Or are they the result of nonsatanic abuse? Are their reports the product of leading questions put to them by biased investigators or frantic parents?

Are the reports of the adults believable? Are their present-day psychological problems the result of satanic abuse? Or are the reports of such abuse symptoms of current psychological problems unrelated to satanic abuse?

Views Opposed to the Idea of a Conspiracy

Many writers, researchers, and professionals are skeptical of satanic ritual abuse evidence. The skeptics make some of the following counterarguments regarding the validity of claims of satanic ritual abuse:

1. There is little physical evidence that adult victims experienced satanic abuse. That is not to say that they were not subjected to childhood abuse. Skeptics merely wonder whether the abuse was of the elaborate, Satan-inspired kind that the victims report.

   For example, even in the study by Young et al. mentioned above involving patients with dissociative disorders, the researchers conceded that the reliability of their evidence and the evidence itself were suspect. They cautioned:

   "It is striking that the patient group reported many similar experiences despite coming from diverse areas, being treated in different locations, and having minimal contact with each other. *Unfortunately, the present study does not rule out the possibility that these patients had read non-professional literature describing reports of satanic cult activity and ritual childhood abuse. They could have incorporated certain incidents from articles or books as 'pseudomemories,' and retrieved them with the same conviction as real memories . . . "* (italics added). In other words, it is possible that the patients had read magazine or newspaper accounts of satanic activity and recounted the stories to the researchers as if they were their own memories.

   The researchers added that "hard evidence in support of the patient reports was difficult to secure."

2. Many adults who claim to have been victims of satanic ritual abuse suffer severe psychological disorders. They may give conflicting accounts, although in a very convincing fashion. In Hicks's article, police investigators admit that it may take years to piece together a coherent story from a victim. Many agree that these adults could well be victims of sexual abuse, but whether the abuse was satanically inspired is unclear.

3. In the article "Satanic, Occult, and Ritualistic Crime: A Law-Enforcement Perspective," Kenneth Lanning, an expert on child abuse and a former FBI Supervisory Special Agent, points out that not one investigation by the FBI or by local police departments has documented a case of satanic murder, cannibalism, or sacrifice.

Dr. Frank Putnam agrees that the lack of evidence makes it difficult to accept the conspiracy theory. He wonders how such bloody rituals avoid detection: If torture and cannibalism are occurring, why has none of this blood and gore been turned up in investigations? No evidence been discovered in the United States, and investigators in England and the Netherlands have also come up empty-handed. Putnam maintains that it is virtually impossible to keep a widespread conspiracy network secret. Furthermore, violent or very deviant organizations (such as the Nazi party in Germany) tend to collapse of themselves. Why, Dr. Putnam wonders, would a satanic network be immune from disintegration?

4. In the same article, Dr. Putnam quotes a U.S. Department of Justice estimate that between fifty-two and 158 children are kidnapped and murdered by strangers per year. While still a chilling statistic, this estimate conflicts sharply with the belief that thousands of children are allegedly kidnapped and sacrificed in satanic ceremonies.

5. A question has been raised regarding some in the mental-health professions who have uncritically accepted the claims made by alleged survivors of satanic ritual abuse. Sociologist Jeffrey Victor, in his article "Satanic Cult 'Survivor' Stories," has suggested that some mental-health professionals have formed their own "closed community": They have become "true believers" in the claims and, rather than trying to validate their stories, have been working to protect them "from the supposed dangers of the satanic-cult conspiracy."

Victor asserts that some mental-health professionals have lost their open-mindedness on the Satanism-abuse issue: "Psychotherapists in the network now accept the satanic-cult stories on the basis of 'faith' alone . . . The 'survivor' stories have now attained the status of taken-for-granted 'reality' . . ."

Conflicting Ideas

Every year a number of children are victims of horrible and unspeakable crimes. Starting early in their lives, many children are severely traumatized by angry, sadistic parents or other adults. But there is little or no evidence to support the claim that thousands and thousands of instances of abuse are related to an organized satanic conspiracy. If that is true, then what is the explanation for these adult "survivor" stories?

Other Possible Explanations

In many cases a patient begins to recall episodes of childhood abuse and victimization while undergoing psychotherapy or hypnosis. She may recall bizarre and ritualistic activities. Often the victim describes mutilations, sexual acts, cannibalism, and ceremonial sacrifices.

Some people have suggested that the memories recovered through psychotherapy may be false memories, recollections of events that never happened, or distorted memories of real events. This raises a difficult issue: For both the patient and the psychotherapist, false memories are virtually indistinguishable from real memories. Often the memories are of events described in great detail and with intense emotion attached to the recollection. It sometimes occurs that a patient recalls memories of abuse in such a matter-of-fact and emotionless manner that mental-health professionals conclude that the person has "dissociated" intellectual knowledge of the abuse from emotional appreciation of its impact as a means of self-preservation.

Other people believe that in many cases of recovered memories, particularly when the patient recalls satanic ritual abuse, the victim may be subtly rewarded by overzealous psychotherapists, social workers, or law-enforcement officials. During psychotherapy, or investigation of abuse, the victim may be unintentionally influenced by a psychotherapist or investigator intent on uncovering ritual cult abuse or satanic or occult activities. The memories "recalled" by these victims may not be real memories.

Many Are Convinced

Without hard physical evidence why do so many people, including law-enforcement officials and mental-health professionals, believe that a tightly organized network of Satanists is committing these crimes? Lanning suggests two reasons for the acceptance of and belief in a satanic conspiracy theory:

"First, it is a simple explanation for a complex problem. Nothing is more simple than 'the devil made them do it.' If we do not understand something, we make it the work of some supernatural force. During the Middle Ages, serial killers were thought to be vampires and werewolves, and child sexual abuse was the work of demons taking the form of parents and clergy. It may also help to 'explain' unusual, bizarre, and compulsive sexual urges and behavior.

"Second, the conspiracy theory is a popular one. We find it difficult to believe that one bizarre individual could commit a crime we find so offensive."

The idea that false memories of satanic ritual abuse may be planted, even unintentionally, by psychotherapists or investigators is a controversial one. However, most members of the mental-health profession as well as law-enforcement officials believe that there is a middle ground; they believe that some of what the victims allege may be true and accurate, but some recalled memories may be distorted. The challenge is to determine which is which. It is most likely that victims who recall satanic ritual abuse were in fact victims of some form of abuse or trauma.

Psychiatry and a Satanic Conspiracy

Several years ago, a new area of psychiatric practice was developed that dealt specifically with issues of satanic cult conspiracy but from a different angle. The diagnosis and treatment were not widely adopted, but the treatment was used in a number of psychiatric facilities. The treatment was not for victims of ritual cult abuse who had recovered memories. Instead it focused on treating people who did not have any memories of having been part of a satanic network but who were told that they had in fact participated in such a network as members.

These individuals were seen by psychiatrists, who diagnosed them as suffering from multiple personality disorder (MPD). The reason, the psychiatrists explained to them and their families, was because the patients had been part of a cult even though they did not have any memories of it. They were told that they may have participated in satanic rituals, including ritual sacrifice and other horrors. Usually the patient and her family were warned that if the patient did not now free herself of that satanic association with the help of psychiatry, she would inflict the same indoctrination on her children.

Not surprisingly, many people did have themselves hospitalized. Some such patients were then given drug treatment, put under hypnosis, physically restrained for hours at a time, and interrogated repeatedly about their satanic connections.

Ultimately, most if not all such programs were stopped. Some questioned their effectiveness, and others expressed concern over harm that may have been inflicted on patients.

In the *Chicago Tribune*, writer Ted Gregory recounted a court case concerning this type of treatment. An Illinois woman sued her former psychiatrist for malpractice. In her lawsuit, she alleged "psychological torture" as the result of having false memories implanted into her mind through the suggestions and hypnosis of a psychiatrist. These implanted memories included her supposed participation in the sexual assault of her children and in a satanic cult that kidnapped and cannibalized children. In 1997 the court found in her favor. She was awarded more than $10 million.

This case is one of several in recent years where payments have been ordered to patients after courts found mental-health professionals guilty of implanting false memories. It suggests that at times, even for experienced and prominent mental-health workers, the line between mental-health issues and perceived ritual or satanic activity can become blurred.

Lured into Satanism

It is important to think carefully about Satanism instead of taking what people say about it at face value. The emotional nature of Satanism and the media attention directed to it can make it easy to overlook the facts. In addition, if a friend or acquaintance whom you admire says that Satanism is okay, why not try it? that may make it appealing. Take time to form your own opinions on the basis of fact.

The following statements will help you assess whether you or someone you know may be vulnerable to being recruited into Satanism.

1. My parents often ignore me or just don't pay enough attention to me, and that upsets me.

2. I want to experiment with drugs, but I'm afraid of being caught.

3. I was physically or sexually abused as a child.

4. I have been robbed or beaten up.

5. It is not unusual to see violence in my neighborhood.

6. My parents make me go to church, and I really resent it.

7. Adults do not seem to understand my taste in music.

8. My parents have given me too many rules, and I feel angry about that.

9. I don't feel good enough about myself to ask a special boy/girl on a date. I wish I could do something about it. I feel hopeless.

10. I spend a lot of time playing Dungeons and Dragons or similar games.

11. A lot of emphasis is placed on religion in our house, but my parents don't practice what they preach.

12. I feel good when I can do something outrageous that disturbs adults.

If you agreed with a lot of these statements, it is important to think carefully about how you can cope with and express your feelings in a healthy way.

Recruitment

Many methods are used to lure young people into joining satanic groups. Sometimes the appeal is to curiosity, at other times to the carnal, fun-loving side of life or to the promise of having power. Still other methods involve manipulative and criminal activities. Recruitment is usually very subtle and can seem innocent. You can become deeply involved quickly without realizing that you have joined.

The Appeal

Generally, the initial approach to a potential recruit is low-key. A person might be invited to a meeting on an intriguing topic. Think for a moment what subjects you might be curious about. What about witchcraft, or explaining unusual occurrences? How about demonic possession and exorcism? The millennium? If you play board games such as Dungeons and Dragons, would you like to learn more about how to win? The goal of this approach is to get the person alone with a Satanist in order to begin psychological manipulation.

Early recruiting efforts might also involve an appeal to the fun-loving side of a person. Parties are used to recruit people into Satanism. Parties offer abundant alcohol, illegal drugs, and uninhibited sex. Would you be tempted to go to such a party if you were promised that no one would find out? Are you curious about what it would be like to use drugs, especially if you were promised that it was safe? If you were told that a very special boy or girl would be at the party and would show you a good time, would you be tempted? Recruitment methods like these are effective because they seem to promise the fulfillment of wants and desires with no strings attached.

The Next Phase

These lures may then be followed by more manipulative techniques of recruitment.

Addiction. Drawing a prospect into addiction to alcohol or drugs can be a tool to ensure participation. You might be given a drug for free until you are hooked on it, and then be required to pay for it or do something in exchange. This might involve securing animals for sacrifice, helping to recruit others, or engaging in criminal activity to help support a satanic group.

Blackmail is also used in recruitment to Satanism. Police report that sexually explicit photographs are sometimes used. At parties, prospects are made to get drunk or high on drugs, and then photographed in a compromising position, perhaps with a member of the opposite sex or the same sex. They are then threatened with exposure to family, friends, and others unless they join the Satan worshipers.

Brainwashing and hypnosis are also used for recruitment purposes. Prospective members may be told that meditation would free them from the pressures of life. While they are in the meditative state, subtle suggestions are made that encourage participation in Satanism: "I know someone who wants to free you from guilt"; "Power can be achieved through worshiping the Prince of Darkness"; or "Life's purpose is to have fun, and Satan wants to fulfill all your needs." Of course, such suggestions do not guarantee that people will join. They may only cause them to think about it. Another suggestion might be that joining would result in better meditation and even more freedom from stress.

The promise of power may also be used in recruitment to Satanism. You might be told that as a member of the group you can achieve your dreams of success through Satan's powers. Through magic, you can tap into his power and use it for whatever end you desire. For people who have little success in life and who feel hopeless or lonely, this can be a strong influence. How about you? If you were promised fame and fortune, would you join? If you were told that all you had to do was ask, could someone recruit you?

It may well be that some people recruit for what they believe are honest spiritual beliefs. Typically, however, people involved in Satanism because of their spiritual beliefs do not go out of their way to recruit members, according to Kahaner. If you are being actively recruited to become involved in Satanism, be cautious and think it through before agreeing to any participation.

Taking Care of Yourself

Recruitment methods vary for each group and each prospect. What works for one person may not work for another, and not all those who are recruited do join. With some people, however, little effort is needed. What would it take to recruit you? Would what you gained be worth what you gave up? These are difficult questions to answer. Think about it. Don't consider only immediate gains, but also long-term effects: Five years, ten, even twenty years from now, how could it affect your life?

If you find that you are attracted to Satanism, it is a good idea to talk to someone you trust. Find a level-headed adult who will listen. If you can't find an adult, talk with another teen whom you respect and who is respected by others. Tell that person what has happened and what you are thinking and feeling. Talking about problems will help you understand your feelings and clarify your thinking.

A good resource is the guidance counselor or social worker in your school; he or she is trained to listen and help you sort through your feelings. You may find that the real issue is not Satanism at all but your frustration over family conflicts, worry about the future, or feelings of worthlessness. Such feelings are not uncommon.

Talking about them with someone you can rely on to listen helps.

If the idea of talking to someone about feeling attracted to Satanism concerns you because you are fairly certain that that person will encourage you not to get involved in Satanism, and you want to, pay attention. When we want to hide a fact about ourselves, it is sometimes because we know that what we are thinking of doing is not good for us.

Characteristics of Teens at Risk

In their article "Psychological Dynamics of Adolescent Satanism," psychologist Moriarty and Police Chief Donald Story argue that vulnerability to Satanism may begin as early as childhood. They suggest that poor parenting styles may put some children at risk, and they point to three aspects of parent-child interactions that may present problems. Remember, however, that just because parents and children have one, two, or all three of these problems doesn't mean that the children will become involved in Satanism. It only means they are more likely to do so than someone without these difficulties.

The first problem is emotional withdrawal of parents at critical times in children's lives. Some parents are cold by nature and do not give support to their children. They may be too preoccupied with their own problems to be available for their children. In such cases, the children may seek other ways to find the acceptance they need.

For example, suppose you are seven years old and bring home a special project from school. What would you want your parents to say? Probably something like, "That is really pretty" or "You must have worked hard on that." But what if they say, "That's stupid" or "Who cares?"—or even worse, ignore you and throw away your project? You wanted to please your parents and win their praise, but instead you faced rejection, coldness, and criticism. If such interactions happen often enough, Moriarty and Story believe, the children are at greater risk of being attracted to Satanism.

A second problem that puts children at risk is early experiences with violence, either as observer or victim. Exposure to violence is one predictor of violent behavior in young people; violence tends to lose its sensationalism and to be a part of daily life. Since Satanism uses forms of violence—for example, sacrifice—teenagers previously exposed to violence are less likely to find it repulsive.

Think how much violence you are exposed to every day. Television and movies have significant amounts and varieties of violence. What about the newspapers, with stories of murder and rape? Now imagine that you live in a place where violent acts take place in your home or neighborhood. What if your parents abused you? It is not surprising that children who live in such conditions are at greater risk of becoming involved in Satanism.

A third parent-child interaction that increases risk is when parents demand strict religious observance while violating the rules themselves. Why is this?

It is believed that as children grow older they seek a way to ease the guilt feelings that often come from normal development. These feelings may arise from sexual urges due to maturation, the need to develop an identity apart from the parents, or rebellion against authority and conformity. Contradictory behavior by the parents, then, only causes confusion. The normal guilt feelings are not easily resolved by the religious system preached by the parents. By encouraging acting-out behavior, indulgence of sexual desires, and an egocentric view of the universe, Satanism offers a convenient way to absolve feelings of guilt.

Several other factors may put teenagers at risk for Satanism, according to J. Mercer, author of *Behind the Mask of Adolescent Satanism.* These factors include low self-esteem, alienation from others, and curiosity about sex and drugs. A typical profile of a teenager involved in Satanism is white, middle-class, average to above average in intelligence, and a loner. At-risk teenagers are probably having problems at home and are unable to talk with their parents or other supportive adults. They may also lack a sense of positive and healthy morality. Young people with these characteristics are vulnerable, but that does not mean they will become involved in Satanism.

Music

The controversy over music with grim or satanic verses is widely debated. Groups such as the Parents' Music Resource Center believe that this music is the primary reason for problems in today's young people. Thomas W. Wedge, author of the *The Satan Hunter,* claims that heavy-metal music is the fundamental recruiting method for Satanism and that it promotes deepening involvement. In his articles "Heavy Metal: A New Religion" and "Heavy Metal Music and Drug Abuse in Adolescents," psychiatrist Paul King expresses deep concern over heavy metal. He states that it represents a public-health problem serious enough to warrant some type of control. Although he does not advocate censorship, Dr. King does think that heavy-metal music should be labeled as potentially harmful to health. Dr. King's concern is that some teenagers are so caught up in their headlong rush toward maturity and so conscious of peer pressure that they are especially sus-ceptible to the violent or satanic suggestions in some heavy-metal music. However, these explanations fail to take into account possible emotional issues that may cause some to become involved in Satanism while others do not.

To the question, "Does listening to heavy-metal or industrial rock music mean that you are at risk for becom-ing involved in Satanism?" the answer is yes and no. There is no conclusive evidence that listening to such music means that you will become involved in Satanism. Psychologists and researchers in Satanism agree that many other factors must be considered. In fact, some of them say that few listeners even pay attention to the lyrics.

Probably the most important consideration is the emo-tional state of the listener. For most generally well-adjusted teenagers, listening to heavy-metal music will likely cause damage only to the eardrums if listened to at high volume. However, the music may attract some teenagers who are having serious emotional conflicts. Such conflicts may make them more susceptible to sug-gestion and therefore more likely to be recruited to Satanism. For these teens, violent suggestions in the lyrics of heavy-metal or industrial rock music may be dangerous. Being more vulnerable, they may be influenced into criminal behaviors and possibly suicide.

So the question is: Is it more important to censor music lyrics, or to address the needs of young people who are experiencing emotional conflicts?

What Do You Think?

What about you? Are you at risk? Take a few minutes to review the statements on pages 76–77. Did you agree with many of them? A few, some, most? The more yes agreements, the more you are at risk. Remember, however, that having some of these characteristics does not mean that you will become involved in Satanism. *You always have other choices.* If you are concerned or worried, find someone to talk with, someone that you trust, who can help you think through what this means. If possible, find someone who is knowledgeable about Satanism. A good choice would be your school counselor, principal, or a respected teacher. It is important to have as much information as possible before making a decision. Think about the long-term impact rather than gratifying short-term desires.

Have you been approached by someone involved in Satanism? Are you tempted to join? Answer the three following questions. This will help you avoid making a wrong decision:

- "Why am I tempted?" List your reasons, and be honest with yourself. Are your reasons positive and healthy, or are they destructive?

- "What are my long-term goals for five years from now? ten years? twenty years?" If you don't have long-term goals, talk with someone to help you develop them. They may involve education, career issues, desire for a family, or health concerns. Will Satanism further or impede your reaching these goals?

↪ "How do I feel about myself? Am I a worthwhile person?" If your answer is that you feel worthless, hopeless, lonely, or discouraged, Satanism will not solve the problem. Talking to someone—a teacher, friend, parent, or counselor—can help.

Signs of Involvement: Mike

Various authors and publications point to supposed "markers" of satanic dabbling. A short list compiled from two such sources follows:

↝ Noticeable changes in behavior such as withdrawing from family and friends or showing intense anger at family.

↝ Changes in dietary habits.

↝ Steep drop in grades.

↝ Abuse of drugs or alcohol.

↝ Marks such as tattoos, skin mutilations, or a blackened fingernail, often on the little finger of the left hand.

↝ Possession of ritual objects such as a black-covered diary.

↝ Use of a satanic nickname.

↝ Appearance of odd alphabetic or satanic symbols on clothing or in notebooks.

Other signs to watch for are unhappiness with life and direct or indirect references to suicide and death.

What do these signs of involvement mean? Some people fear that the mixture of satanic worship and teenage rebelliousness will result in commission of illegal or immoral acts. Sociologist Dr. David Bromley notes that even though stories of teenage participation in satanic rituals and sacrifices may be exaggerated, there is a high level of alienation and gloominess within many young people's lives.

The Case of Mike

Mike's parents, Don and Shirley, sat quietly waiting to see the principal. This was the first time they had been called by the school, so they weren't sure what to expect. All they knew was that the principal wanted to see them about Mike's "attitude." They both were aware of changes in their son's behavior, so they weren't surprised that the teachers also had noticed.

Mike's personality had undergone a dramatic alteration over the past two months. He had grown even more indifferent about school, and his attendance had dropped. For years, Mike had been shy and a loner and had spent most evenings closed off in his room. But now he was always going out with a group of friends whom his parents didn't know. They began to worry when these "outings" lasted until early morning.

There were other changes, too. Posters appeared in his room depicting grotesque satanic scenes. He bought CDs that his parents considered disturbing. Mike's father tried to reassert his authority, but Mike refused to take the posters down or to stop listening to the music. One day Mike came home wearing an upside-down cross earring. Angry words were exchanged, and Mike stormed out of the house.

The principal now invited Mike's parents into her office. Once all were seated, she began: "I'm glad you were able to come on such short notice, but we need to discuss your son's behavior. Mike's teachers have become very concerned about him. They say he has become argumentative in class and that he manifests both a great deal of anger and a low sense of self-esteem. I tried to talk with him several times, but he just tuned me out. Actually, his tone was downright disrespectful. Then yesterday, he turned in this poem to Mrs. Harvey, his English teacher." The principal handed Mike's parents a paper:

DEATH BECOMES HER
by Mike T.

On an altar of sacrifice
Waiting to die,
Lay beaten and bleeding
A virgin in white.
"I've brought you your victim,"
Said I to my Lord,
"Now grant me my due,
And prepare me a palace
By Hell's darkest tarn."

Mike's parents couldn't read on. They were overcome with surprise and disgust, appalled by the drawings Mike used to illustrate his poem—

depictions of Satan and a battered, brutalized female figure. They became gripped by the realization of what they were seeing. Finally, Mike's father muttered: "We didn't know Mike was into this devil worship. We just didn't know."

There was much that Mike's parents did not know. For years, they had been defeated by his uncooperativeness and lack of ambition. They had tried coaxing, then shaming, and even bribing him to behave more responsibly and to have some ambition. Eventually, they gave up, concluding that if he didn't want to take responsibility, they wouldn't give him any. The result was a vicious circle: The more his parents wrote him off as lazy and stubborn, the more sullen and withdrawn Mike became.

Mike's parents did not know where Mike and his new friends went or what they did. They would not have suspected the destination to be an abandoned pavilion in a forest preserve. Nor would they have suspected that Mike and his friends used marijuana and alcohol, lit candles, and read from a satanic ritual book. They wouldn't have guessed in a million years that Traci, a vacant-eyed sophomore at Mike's school, was part of the group and engaged in sexual acts with Mike and his friends.

They did not know that Mike had participated in criminal acts with his friends. He had spray-painted swastikas and satanic symbols on garage doors and on gravemarkers in a cemetery. He had helped to distract the sales clerk as his friends stole several hundred dollars' worth of jewelry to use in their ceremonies. It was Mike who had set a ceremonial fire in a toolshed, burning it down. If Mike's parents had investigated Mike's bedroom, they would have come across a stash of books on Satanism that Mike had stolen from the public library. He kept these books along with his own Book of Shadows, *a journal containing hateful poems dedicated to the homage of Satan and threats against Mike's "enemies."*

His parents did not know what kind of gratification Mike obtained from involvement in satanic rituals. They did not know how he had become involved in the first place. And they had no clue as to the implications of his involvement.

What made the deepest impact on Mike's parents was the principal's urging them to get Mike professional help. In the car on their way home, Mike's mother mentioned a local hospital that specialized in treating troubled adolescents. "Perhaps," she said as she dabbed tears from her eyes, "the doctors at the hospital could turn Mike around." She feared that might be the only choice. Don agreed. He would find out from his company whether his health insurance would cover such treatment.

This hypothetical case raises a number of questions about satanic involvement.

What factors were critical in initially steering Mike toward Satanism?

Mike was characterized as a loner. He never seemed sure about his life goals or who he was as a person, and his unstable behavior communicated this uncertainty to schoolmates, teachers, and relatives. The personality he displayed to the world appeared first tentative and apologetic, then hostile and brooding. If they could have found the words, his schoolmates might have given Mike this feedback: If you don't hold yourself in high regard, how do you expect to get any respect from us?

Mike had been mostly written off by his parents. They had given up trying to get through to him. For years they had encouraged him to be more ambitious, outgoing, and responsible. They had tried coaxing, teasing, threatening, and bribing. For example, they had set up a "money for chores" incentive system, but it had a reverse psychological effect: When it dawned on Mike that his parents were trying to "buy" his cooperation, instead of encouraging him, the tactic discouraged him.

By the time Mike was in junior high school, he and his parents battled over control issues: curfew, dress style, spending money, grades and homework, MTV, and cigarette smoking. Mike felt that his parents were dictating to him, that he had no say in the decisions. He was supposed to "like it or lump it,"as he had been told. Mike seethed inside, vowing that the time would come when *he* would take control and do what *he* wanted.

Mike's impaired social and family adjustment appears to be a significant factor in his turning toward Satanism. Parental abuse was not a factor in his case, but it has been associated with satanic preoccupation in other teenagers. It was relevant, for instance, in the case of Traci, the girl who acts out sexually with Mike's group. Traci's parents (both alcoholics) beat her with belts and electrical extension cords in attempts to "discipline" her.

Traci thought seriously about running away or even committing suicide. Eventually, she found a niche in the satanic group; it appealed to her fantasies of escape and excitement.

Some teenagers are attracted to Satanism because the possession of arcane knowledge sets them apart from their peers. It enables them to feel superior to and more powerful than the "uninitiated." However, this factor was not much of a motivator for Mike. Part of his attraction to industrial rock, satanic symbolism, and the grotesque was their disturbing effect on his parents, who were visibly upset. Mike began to adopt satanic symbols and terminology and a gothic clothing style because they were a ready-made identity for him. They represented a way to stake out a "personal territory." He had only vague notions of what Satanism was all about, but he knew that the notions were his and his parents couldn't take them away. At least he could control what he thought and believed.

How did Mike first get mixed up with a group of Satanic dabblers?

Mike's attention had been attracted by a sales clerk at the audio/video store. He was a fellow in his late teens or early twenties (his indeterminate age was part of the mysterious aura about him) who went by the name of Zeta, the sixth letter of the Greek alphabet. Zeta's personal style greatly impressed Mike. With customers, he displayed a subtly condescending attitude. On the surface he appeared helpful and knowledgeable, but an underlying edge to both his voice and body language was mocking, sarcastic, and superior.

The relationship between Mike and Zeta began to grow when Mike innocently inquired about the black polish on Zeta's left little fingernail. As time went by, Zeta let Mike in on his satanic beliefs and the activities of his network of six "co-worshipers." Finally, when Zeta invited Mike to one of their ceremonies, Mike jumped at the chance. No one ever invited him anywhere.

What motivated Mike to become more and more involved with Zeta and his group?

Excitement, pure and simple, won Mike over at first. He found the secret ceremonies frightening, yet exhilarating. He felt, in a way, freed by the negativism of the rituals and the "do-your-own-thing" belief system.

It was this belief system that intensified Mike's irresponsible behavior: Everything that he had been taught was "bad" was now okay. As Mike took the beliefs to heart, a curious cycle was put into motion: The guilt that he might be expected to feel as a result of his drug and alcohol use, his sexual behavior toward Traci, and his anti-Christian values was removed by an "absolving (forgiving) mechanism": The more seriously he believed the satanic message, the easier it became to justify his behavior and to rationalize away the guilt.

What made Mike particularly susceptible to Satanic involvement?

As a "loner," he had few friends and none to whom he was especially close. Some mental health professionals say that people without friends are naturally more at risk. Mike had no one to act as a sounding board for his feelings and ideas.

Friends supply us with corrective feedback. The normal give-and-take of friendship helps us keep a perspective on who we are. Mike lacked self-corrective feedback.

In addition, his relationship with his parents was not positive enough to counterbalance the power he thought he could obtain through satanic dabbling.

What might cause Mike to disengage himself from his cult practices?

Dabblers sometimes abandon their satanic belief system when the stakes become too high. When thefts, drug use, and other criminal acts escalate in frequency and intensity, some people "drop out" because of fear. The dropping out may take the form of an attempt at suicide or a request for hospitalization.

In Mike's case, a concerned teacher noticed his erratic behavior and was sensitive to the satanic themes in his schoolwork. She and his parents were able to discuss the matter with him before he had reached the "drop out" stage.

The Aftermath

Mike's parents followed up their meeting with the principal with a telephone call to a community mental-health agency. They were referred to a counselor experienced in working with teenagers and their families on the conflicts associated with satanic dabbling.

Meeting with Mike's parents, the counselor advised them not to confront Mike with their anger, disappointment, and disgust. Instead, the counselor suggested that they inquire of Mike—in a fact-finding rather than punitive way—

about his interest in Satanism. They were to approach the situation as a problem to be solved, not something for which Mike should be punished.

The counselor also suggested to Mike's parents that they try to listen and to understand while at the same time withholding judgment. Through inquiring, listening, and understanding, bridges could be built between parents and son.

Don and Shirley needed to pose a number of questions to Mike, and to listen carefully and nonjudgmentally to his responses:

- How had he become acquainted with his new "friends"?

- How had he come to trust these cult friends?

- What were the key elements of his new beliefs?

- How deeply involved was he in these beliefs?

- How certain was he that these beliefs reflected his true feelings?

- Was he a different person now? A happier person? Was he more (or less) self-accepting now?

- What important insights did he have now? What had he learned that was of lasting value?

- How was he managing to reconcile his current and former values?

↪ How would he describe himself so that others might better understand his interests, goals, and motivations?

Giving Mike an opportunity to communicate with them—to tell his story and have them listen noncritically—was the first step in the conciliation process. Mike's parents needed to demonstrate that they were trying to understand; at this crucial time, Mike needed to feel listened to and to have a chance to tell his story.

The counselor suggested that Mike needed to know that others cared about him. The counselor was talking about a special kind of caring.

Mike's parents had tried for years to show Mike that they cared. When they yelled at him or criticized him or used shaming tactics to motivate him, they were really trying to show that they cared about him and wanted him to be his best. Now they would have to demonstrate caring through different channels: respect, listening, and encouraging Mike's interests, talents, and goals.

The counselor recommended that Mike's parents not confiscate Mike's posters, CDs, or books, which would set off more ill will over the issue of control. The counselor made the exception that if they discovered such things as stolen merchandise or drugs, they might turn them over to the authorities.

The counselor also recommended family counseling in addition to individual counseling for Mike. It was stressed to Mike's parents that Mike was not to be made the scapegoat for problems that affected the whole family. It was a family system that needed changing, not an individual that needed to be "straightened out."

In his own counseling, Mike would discuss and discover less destructive ways to improve his self-esteem and to achieve a sense of personal mastery. To do this would involve building a network of new friends and finding activities at which Mike excelled. His school counselor was available to help him develop this plan.

Getting Free

In the last chapter we met Mike, a high school student who had become involved in Satanism. A counselor suggested ways for Mike's parents to resolve the impasse. But what about Mike? What could he do to get out of Satanism? How could he help himself?

What if you, like Mike, are involved in Satanism and now want out? What can you do to help yourself? We know that once involved it is difficult to stop. We know that you may be pressured to remain involved even to the point of being blackmailed. You may be embarrassed or ashamed to admit your participation. You may even be afraid of what might happen to you, especially if illegal activities have occurred. Getting out of Satanism is not easy, and it takes courage. But you do not have to go it alone. You can find help.

There are several steps you can take to escape the trap of Satanism. Although it may be difficult, it can be done. Many others have overcome the obstacles that you face.

Remember the reasons why Mike or you might have gotten involved in Satanism. Young people may become involved because they:

➵ feel lonely or shy

➵ feel guilty about their sexual urges

☞ are curious about drugs and alcohol

☞ want to shock adults

☞ want to rebel against authority

☞ come from home situations that are not healthy

☞ are exposed repeatedly to acts of violence

With those reasons in mind, let's see what you can do to help yourself.

1. Find one person who is willing to help you in your struggle. Don't go it alone.

The person you choose should be sensible, approachable, and trustworthy. You do not want to talk to someone who will get hysterical and overreact to what you say. You want a person who will listen quietly and patiently, not automatically judge you. A good choice is a counselor. Counselors are trained to listen and to be open-minded. If you cannot talk to a counselor, however, a respected teacher or other adult is a possibility.

The person should be regularly available to you. At first, you may need to talk frequently. As you work to separate yourself from Satanism, you will need help to overcome its lure.

The person should also be totally trustworthy. You may disclose things that are embarrassing, shameful, and humiliating. Ethical standards require counselors to maintain confidentiality. Except with written permission, they cannot reveal anything you tell them. The only exceptions are child abuse or if you are at risk of hurting yourself or someone else.

Before talking to the chosen person, practice what you want to say. You may want to write it down and rehearse it a few times. Be honest with yourself. Talk about your feelings and thoughts and how they are affecting your life.

2. Learn to appreciate yourself for who you are instead of condemning yourself for not measuring up.

Boosting your level of self-esteem is a key ingredient in your recovery. A good start in building self-esteem is learning about the process of maturing into young adulthood. Young people tend to believe that what they are experiencing is abnormal or that no one else could possibly feel or think the way they do. Yet experience shows that these feelings and urges are normal and to be expected. Understanding this will not automatically result in understanding yourself nor in ending your involvement in Satanism. But knowing that you are not alone and that your experience is part of the maturing process can give you strength as you terminate your involvement.

Ask yourself:

> *"Did I get involved because of curiosity or the novelty of it?"* If so, that is normal; you should be curious. You are stimulated constantly by the world around you and need to satisfy your curiosity.

> *"Did I join to satisfy my sexual desires?"* In adolescence, your body experiences rapid and drastic

changes. Coping with these changes requires an effort. Feeling guilty about these urges may put you at risk of being lured into satanic worship. Recognize that your feelings and desires are normal, not reasons for guilt.

"Did I want attention?" Everyone wants to be noticed. No one wants to be the last person picked for a team or left out of the social scene. Was the person whose attention you sought an adult or one of your peers? Did you join to rebel against authority figures? Wanting attention and chafing at authority are part of normal development. Once you understand that you are not alone, you can find other, more appropriate ways to gain attention.

You may also want to ask a counselor or psychologist about the importance of having a healthy level of self-esteem. One of these helping professionals may have concrete suggestions for how you can learn to value yourself. Increased self-esteem should help you get out and stay out of satanic worship.

One method of enhancing your self-esteem is by keeping a journal. All you need is a notebook and a pen. Through a journal, you can find an outlet for your hopes, plans, conflicts, and decisions. Your journal might have several topic headings. In a section titled, "Who I Am," you can write about your wishes and dreams; your career or educational goals and aspirations; the qualities or characteristics you would like to develop; how you can cope positively with a crisis or interpersonal conflict; your favorite memories; and special qualities of yours that can make a positive difference for others.

Another section of your journal could be titled, "What I Want to Change About Me." Here you could talk to your-self about behaviors that you would like to increase or decrease and work out specific steps to achieve your goal. For example, you might want to increase the time you spend with a favorite relative or to decrease how much you gossip about friends.

Dr. Patricia Peterson-Sanborn, in her unpublished work "Personality Type of Adolescents and Type of Imaged Personal Heroines," reminds us how important heroic figures are in our personal lives. She notes that heroes and heroines serve as sources of inspiration as well as role mod-els. We all admire someone for his or her qualities, charac-teristics, or deeds. Many young people have sport figures as personal heroes; Michael Jordan is currently popular in that category. Many are impressed with the deeds of historical figures such as Martin Luther King, Jr., John F. Kennedy, or Joan of Arc. Thus, another topic for your journal could be your personal heroes. Think about whom you admire and why. What qualities of these heroes and heroines impress you? What message do they have about how your life could be more satisfying or enriching?

3. Avoid putting yourself in situations that you identify with Satanism.

In suggestion #2 we talked about raising your level of self-esteem. You also need to work on how other people see you. In our society, people tend to be stereotyped. If your dress style suggests Satanism, people automatically assume that you are involved in it. Therefore you need to build a new identity from the outside in; that is, alter how others see you. There are two basic ways of doing this: first, taking control of your environment, and second, changing your appearance.

You might be tempted to return to Satanism unless you take active control of your environment. Instead of hanging out with your former companions, take steps to find new friends and acquaintances. Pay attention to cues that might cause you to slip back into Satanism. If a certain kind of music makes you think of it, avoid listening to it for at least six months. If certain types of clothing identify you with Satanism or make you think about it, make the appropriate change. Change whatever it is in your surroundings that makes you think about Satanism.

Try also to alter your appearance so that others will see a new you. If you had been wearing only black to signify Satanism, wear clothes that vary in color. If you had been wearing jewelry identified with Satanism, such as an upside-down cross, change this also. If you are serious about wanting to establish a new identity, you need to take drastic steps.

4. Gather information about Satanism from reputable sources.

Read all you can about the subject. Gather information from as many sources as possible. Reading this book is a start. Go to your school or public library and read what others have to say. Several sources of additional information are listed at the end of this book that can help you develop a deeper understanding of Satanism. Read all the material critically. Ask yourself whether it sensationalizes Satanism or treats it rationally. Is it based on fact or fiction? Is it objective and scientific, or subjective fantasy? The more information you have, the better you will be able to stop your involvement in satanic worship.

5. Set short-term and long-term goals.

A problem with some teens who are involved in Satanism is that they have no goals or plans for their life. They live for immediate gratification. One way to help get out of Satanism is setting attainable goals.

Ask yourself what you want out of life. Most young people answer that a wife or husband and family, a good job, a nice house, and good health represent the good things in life. What are your goals? Take a few minutes and think about your goal for one year from now. Two years from now. Five years. Ten years.

Five-year and ten-year goals call for setting short-term goals as well. For example, if your ten-year goal is becoming a lawyer or a doctor, your short-term goal must be to graduate from high school. You might also want to have a short-term goal of improving your grades so you can go to a particular college. Ask yourself: How can I reach my goals? Do you need to do better in high school so you can be accepted in college. Or do you want to attend a trade school? What does it take to be accepted there? Where do you want to live? What will it take to afford an average house in that location? Setting these goals will provide a direction that should help in your struggle to put Satanism behind you.

Choosing New Ideas

Satanism promotes as virtues behaviors that are opposed to what is generally considered healthy, decent behavior. It approves values that directly contradict the teachings of many established religions and that frequently result in harm to oneself or others. It is reasonable, then, that exposing yourself to values that result in benefit to yourself and others may well help you get free from Satanism. Learning about a life-affirming faith or philosophy can go a long way in helping you redefine your views.

If you want to know more about a philosophy or faith, look in the library and talk to adults who are trustworthy. You can choose better alternatives.

Glossary

altar Place of worship, made of wood or stone, often depicted with a nude woman lying on it between two black candles.

amulet Object worn to ward off evil influences; examples include rings, scarabs, stones, animal teeth, ivory phalli, and plants.

arcane Mysterious, obscure.

Athame Ceremonial knife.

Baphomet Idol worshiped at the Black Mass, generally the skull of a goat or other animal.

Beelzebub Satan or the devil in the New Testament; meaning Lord of Flies.

black magic Magic practiced by those in league with the devil; a type of witchcraft.

Black Mass Travesty of the Roman Catholic Mass in which all observances are to Satan.

chalice Cup or goblet used in services.

charm Object worn for magical effect.

consecrate To make, declare, or set apart an object as sacred.

coven Assembly of witches, usually thirteen.

cult Body of beliefs and rituals associated with a particular person or object; a group of people strongly committed to a system of beliefs.

demon An evil spirit; one of Satan's fallen angels.

divination Foretelling the future by occult powers.

doctrine A principle, or statement of ideas or opinions, presented for acceptance and belief.

goat's head Symbol for Satan.

incantation Magical words.

Jaina cross Swastika.

Lord of Flies Beelzebub.

magick Occultist's art of controlling events. Spelled with a "k" to distinguish it from sleight-of-hand.

misnomer Name that is not fitting

Neo-Pagan Concerning nature-centered, pantheistic new religions of North America and Europe.

necromancy Communication with the dead.

occult Matters considered to be involve supernatural powers or knowledge of them

pagan Concerning beliefs of a usually pre-Christian religion that is not a dominant religion.

pentagram Five-pointed star, the most important occult symbol.

psychotherapy Treatment of mental or emotional disorder.

Sabbat Midnight meeting of witches and warlocks; believed to be presided over by Satan.

talisman Powerful object, usually an amulet or a trinket.

vampirism Activities associated with living life as a vampire, including drinking of blood, filing of teeth, sleeping during the daytime.

warlock Male witch.

white magic Magic used for benevolent purposes; for healing.

witch Female who practices magic.

Where to Go for Help

If you are involved in Satanism and want help in getting out, or if you believe you may be the survivor of satanic ritual abuse, talk to an adult you trust. A parent, teacher, school counselor, religious leader, therapist, or the parent of a friend may be able to help you. You are not alone. Many people want to assist you.

In addition, the following organizations provide information to the public. Their information varies in quality and may be biased. You must be the judge.

False Memory Syndrome Foundation
3401 Market Street, Suite 130
Philadelphia, PA 19104
(800) 568-8882
(215) 387-1865
Web site: http://iquest.com/~fitz/fmsf/
This organization provides information, such as studies and reports, that is skeptical of claims of recovered memory and conspiracies of widespread satanic ritual abuse.

International Cult Education Program
American Family Foundation
P. O. Box 2265
Bonita Springs, FL 34133
(941) 514-3081

Web site: http://www.csj.org
email: aff@worldnet.att.net
This organization provides information on cults and cult
activities. It offers help to families with cult-affected members
and sponsors workshops for families of members and for former members.

Parents' Music Resource Center
1500 Arlington Boulevard
Arlington, VA 22209
(703) 527-9466
This organization provides information on the content of lyrics
in contemporary music.

Task Force on Missionaries and Cults
Jewish Community Relations Council of New York
111 West 40th Street
New York, NY 10018
(212) 983-4800
email: davcra@aol.com
This organization provides information on cults and cult
activities.

In Canada

Info Cult
Resource Centre on Cultic Thinking
5655 Park Avenue, Suite 208
Montreal, Quebec H2V 4H2
CANADA
(514) 274-2333
This organization has an extensive collection of information
on cults, cultic groups, and related subjects, and works with
members' families in an advisory capacity.

Web Sites

Answers in Action—The Hard Facts About Satanic Ritual Abuse:
http://www.answers.org/Satan/Sra.html

Concerned Citizens for Legal Accountability:
http://www.ags.uci.edu/~dehill/witchhunt/ccla/home.htm

Ontario Consultants on Religious Tolerance:
http://www.religioustolerance.org

Police Social Services Joint Enquiry Team Report (UK):
http://samsara.law.cwru.edu/comp_law/jetrep.htm

The Broxtowe Files (concerning the Joint Enquiry Team Report):
http://www.users.globalnet.co.uk/~dlhed/Default.htm

Witch Hunt Information Center:
http://web.mit.edu/harris/www/witchhunt.html

For Further Reading

This book has summarized and integrated a good deal of information to help you understand some of the issues and problems related to Satanism, but it is by no means comprehensive.

Many of the young people who participate in satanic worship do so not for religious reasons, but for other reasons that vary from person to person. If the sensationalism of Satanism can be set aside, most often you will find troubled, hurting young people involved. If you or someone you know is one of them, you or that person can find the help you, he, or she needs.

You may choose to search for more information on Satanism in your library. It is important, however, to read books and articles on the subject with skepticism. One quick way to judge the quality of the information is by noting the publisher of the book. Is it a reputable publisher? The librarian may be able to tell you whether a particular book is likely to contain unbiased information.

Adler, Margot. *Drawing Down the Moon: Witches, Druids, Goddess Worshippers, and Other Pagans in America Today.* New York: Penguin USA, 1997.

Baskin, Wade. *Satanism: A Guide to the Awesome Power of Satan.* Secaucus, NJ: Citadel Press, 1988.

Beit-Hallahmi, Benjamin. *The Illustrated Encyclopedia of Active New Religions, Sects, and Cults.,* rev. ed. New York: Rosen Publishing Group, 1998.

Bromley, David G., and Susan G. Ainsley. "Satanism and Satanic Churches: The Contemporary Incarnations," in Timothy

Miller, ed., *America's Alternative Religions*. Albany, NY: State University of New York, 1995.

Bourgat, D., A. Gagnon, and J. M. Bradford. "Satanism in a Psychiatric Adolescent Population," *Canadian Journal of Psychiatry*, No. 33, 1988, pp. 197–202.

Cage, R. *"Problems in Multiple Victim Cases,"* presentation to Health Sciences' Response to Child Maltreatment Conference, Children's Hospital, San Diego, January 17–20, 1990.

Cavendish, Richard. *The Black Arts*. New York: Perigree Books, 1988.

Elliott, Lynn C. "Satanic Ritual Abuse and Multiple Personality Disorder," *The Advocate*, No. 15, August 1991.

Fine, Gary Alan, and Jeffrey H. Victor. "Satanic Tourism: Adolescent Dabblers and Identity Work," *Phi Delta Kappan*, September 1994.

Gardner, M. "The Tragedies of False Memories." *Skeptical Inquirer*, No. 18, Fall 1994, pp. 464–470.

Goldstein, Jeffrey H. *Aggression and Crimes of Violence,* 2nd ed. New York: Oxford University Press, 1986.

Griffis, D. W. "A Law Enforcement Primer on Cults." D.W.G. Enterprise Product, a Griffis Publisher, 1985.

Hicks, Robert D. *In Pursuit of Satan: The Police and the Occult*. New York: Prometheus Books, 1991.

———."The Police Model of Satanic Crime," in James T. Richardson, Joel Best, and David G. Bromley, eds. *The Satanism Scare*. New York: Aldine de Gruyter, 1991.

———."Police Pursuit of Satanic Crime, Part I." *Skeptical Inquirer,* Vol. 14, No. 3, Summer 1990, pp. 276–286.

———."Police Pursuit of Satanic Crime, Part II: The Satanic Conspiracy and Urban Legends." *Skeptical Inquirer,* Vol. 14, No. 4, Summer 1990, pp. 378–389.

Jenkins, P., and D. Maier-Katkin, "Occult Survivors: The Making of a Myth," in James T. Richardson, Joel Best, and David G. Bromley, eds., *The Satanism Scare.* New York: Aldine de Gruyter, 1991.

Jones, D. P. H. "Commentary: Ritualism and Child Sexual Abuse," *Child Abuse and Neglect,* No. 15, 1991, pp. 163–170.

Kahaner, Larry. *Cults That Kill.* New York: Warner Books, Inc., 1994.

King, Paul. "Heavy Metal: A New Religion," *Journal of Tennessee Medical Association,* No. 78, 1985, pp. 754–755.

———."Heavy Metal Music and Drug Abuse in Adolescents," *Postgraduate Medicine,* No. 83, 1988, pp. 295–304.

Klaits, Joseph. *Servants to Satan: The Age of Witch Hunts.* Bloomington, IL: Indiana University Press, 1987.

Laboriel, L., C. Gould, D.A. Sexton, M. C. Cioffi, and D. Brown, *"Ritual Abuse."* Los Angeles: Children's Institute International, 1989.

Lanning, Kenneth V. "Satanic, Occult, and Ritualistic Crime: A Law-Enforcement Perspective," *Police Chief,* Vol. 56, No. 10, October 1989, pp. 62–83.

LaVey, Anton S. *The Satanic Rituals.* New York: Avon Books, 1991.

———. *The Satanic Witch* (originally *The Compleat Witch*). Portland, OR: Feral House, 1989.

Loftus, Elizabeth F. "Creating False Memories." *Scientific American,* September 1997, pp. 70–75.

———, and Katherine Ketchum. *The Myth of Repressed Memory: False Memories and Allegations of Sexual Abuse.* New York: St. Martin's, 1996.

Makin, K. *"Satanic Child Abuse Cited by Aid Group,"* Toronto *Globe and Mail,* December 22, 1987, p. A12.

Martin, Daniel, and Gary Alan Fine. "Satanic Cults, Satanic Play: Is 'Dungeons and Dragons' a Breeding Ground for the Devil?" in James T. Richardson, Joel Best, and David G. Bromley, eds., *The Satanism Scare.* New York: Aldine de Gruyter, 1991.

Meade, J. " Satanism," *Teacher Magazine.* September/October, 1991.

Mercer, J. *Behind the Mask of Adolescent Satanism.* Minneapolis, MN: Deaconess Press, 1991.

Miller, Timothy, ed. *America's Alternative Religions.* Albany, NY: State University of New York Press, 1995.

Moriarty, Anthony R. "Adolescent Satanic Cult Dabblers: A Differential Diagnosis," *Journal of Mental Health Counseling,* No. 13,1991, pp. 393–404.

Nathan, Debbie. "Satanism and Child Molestation: Constructing the Ritual Abuse Scare," in James T. Richardson, Joel Best, and David G. Bromley, eds., *The Satanism Scare.* New York: Aldine de Gruyter, 1991.

——— and Michael Snedeker. *Satan's Silence: Ritual Abuse and the Making of a Modern American Witch Hunt.* New York: Basic Books, 1996.

Parents' Music Resource Center. *Let's Talk Rock: A Primer for Parents.* Arlington, VA: Parents' Music Resource Center Press, 1988.

Passantino, Bob and Gretchen. *Satanism. (Zondervan Guide to Cults and Religious Movements.)* Grand Rapids: Zondervan Publishing House, 1995.

Putnam, Frank W. "The Satanic Ritual Abuse Controversy," *Child Abuse and Neglect,* No. 15, 1995, pp. 175–179.

Richardson, James T., Joel Best, and David G. Bromley, eds. *The Satanism Scare*. New York: Aldine De Gruyter, 1991.

Rose, Elizabeth S. [pseudonym] "Surviving the Unbelievable: Cult Ritual Abuse." Ms., January/February 1993, pp. 40–45.

Russell, Jeffrey Burton. *Lucifer: The Devil in the Middle Ages*. Ithaca, NY: Cornell University Press, 1986.

———. *The Prince of Darkness: Radical Evil and the Power of Good in History*. Ithaca, NY: Cornell University Press, 1992.

———. *Satan: The Early Christian Tradition*. Ithaca, NY, and London: Cornell University Press, 1987.

Schacter, Daniel L. *Searching for Memory: The Brain, the Mind, and the Past*. New York: HarperCollins, 1997.

Simandl, Robert J., and B. Maysmith. "Dabbling Their Way to Ritual Crime," *Cult Awareness Network News,* August 1988.

Simon, E. Simon. *Necronomicon*. New York: Avon, 1995.

TerHorst, C. "The Dark Side of Adolescence," *Palatine Daily Herald,* December, 8, 1988.

Victor, Jeffrey S. "Satanic Cult 'Survivor' Stories," *Skeptical Inquirer,* No. 15, 1991, pp. 274–280.

———. *Satanic Panic: The Creation of a Contemporary Legend*. Peru, IL: Open Court, 1993.

———. "The Spread of Satanic-Cult Rumors," *Skeptical Inquirer,* No. 14,1990, pp. 287–291.

Watters, E. "The Devil in Mr. Ingram." *Mother Jones,* Vol. 16, July/August 1991, pp. 30–33+.

Wedge, Thomas W. *The Satan Hunter*. Canton, OH: Daring Books, 1988.

Wheeler, B. R., S. Wood, and R. J. Hatch. "Assessment and Intervention with Adolescents Involved in Satanism," *Social Work,* November–December, 1988, pp. 547–550.

Wright, Lawrence. "Remembering Satan." *The New Yorker,* Vol. 69, May 17, 1993, pp. 60–66+.

————. "Remembering Satan." *The New Yorker,* Vol. 69, May 24, 1993, pp. 54–66+.

Young, W. C., R. G. Sachs, B. G. Braun, and R. T. Watkins. "Patients Reporting Ritual Abuse in Childhood: A Critical Syndrome," *Child Abuse and Neglect,* No. 15, 1991, pp. 181–189.

Index